HANDBOOK
FOR SPIES

HANDBOOK
FOR SPIES

ALEXANDER FOOTE

COACHWHIP PUBLICATIONS
Landisville, Pennsylvania

Handbook for Spies, by Alexander Foote
First published 1949, simultaneous New York and London.
© 2011 Coachwhip Publications

CoachwhipBooks.com

Cover images: Chess pieces © Len Neighbors; Map © Gladwin

ISBN 1-61646-067-9
ISBN-13 978-1-61646-067-9

CONTENTS

1
Entrance to Espionage

It was a perfectly ordinary front door. Its shining brass knocker, its neat but slightly faded green paint did not distinguish it from thousands of others of its kind. But that door was my entrance to espionage. Beyond that door lay the dim passageway leading through a twilight labyrinth of international intrigue. Once past that door, my feet were set on the road which led me to Germany, to Switzerland and a Swiss jail, beyond the Iron Curtain to Moscow, and back again to Berlin and freedom. When the door closed behind me there began a ten-year episode which was to end with my being condemned as a spy by the courts of one country and sentenced to death by the decrees of another.

It was an autumn day in October 1938. The leaves were still on the trees lining that pleasant road in St. John's Wood, and there was still something of summer in the air as I walked toward the house with the green door—the door of the flat where I was to be recruited into the Russian Secret Service.

As a result of my call I was for three vital years of the war a member and, to a large extent, controller of the Russian spy net in Switzerland which was working against Germany. The information passed to Moscow over my secret transmitter affected the course of the war at one of its crucial stages. I was a key link in a network whose lines stretched into the heart of the German high command itself; and it was I who sent back much of the information which enabled the Russians to make their successful stand before Moscow.

This story is entirely factual; every incident and every character is true and genuine. The result may prove disillusioning to those
who believe that every brunette is a spy and every blonde a virtu-
ous woman in distress. Actually, of course, the life of a spy is often
extremely dull and prosaic. It is the ambition of the good spy to be
as inconspicuous and ordinary as possible. Anything out of the
ordinary is liable to attract attention or, worse still, arouse suspicion. A suspected spy is well on the way to being an arrested
spy, so it can be understood why a spy has a liking for the cloak of
mediocrity.

No one trained solely on spy fiction would recognise a spy. It
would be possible to parade the whole of the Swiss network before
such a man and he would not give them a second glance. What was
unusual in wartime Switzerland about a respectable publisher, a
well-known military commentator, and an *embusqué* Englishman?
Yet these three were the essential core of the Russian spy net
against Germany. Nowadays, in peacetime England, the business-
man from Canada, the little tobacconist round the corner, or the
hearty commercial traveller on the eight-fifteen are far more likely
to be Russian spies than any dumb blonde or sinister baron met in
Grand Hotel.

It would be equally wrong to regard every Communist as a paid
and trained member of the Russian Secret Service. Yet it would be
highly injudicious to whisper the secrets of the atom bomb into
the ear of a pretty Party member at a cocktail party. She would
probably pass the information on as a matter of Party discipline,
but she would not be a Russian spy. Spies will have no obvious
links with the Communist Party. If they ever were Communists,
you will find that they dropped out some time ago—at the time of
their recruitment. If this seems unbelievable, it is only necessary
to look at the various Soviet agents mentioned in this book or in
the report of the Canadian spy case. On the face of it they are, or
were, nearly all highly respectable members of society with at most
only vague leftish leanings. The danger of the avowed Communist
lies not in his espionage activities but in his divided loyalty. He is

perfectly prepared to be recruited as an agent or to pass on any information which he thinks the Party should know.

So much for the characteristics, or rather lack of characteristics, of a spy. As regards the work, it is not so full of escapes and hurried journeys as fiction would lead one to imagine. The hours are long, much of the work is monotonous, and the pay is not excessive considering the risks. The only excitement a spy is likely to have is his last, when he is finally run to earth. An emotion similar to that experienced by the fox. We are assured that the fox really likes being hunted. I have been hunted; and though the sensation is certainly acute, I can hardly describe it as pleasant and as a fellow sufferer my sympathies are entirely with the fox.

I have attempted to describe the workings of a Soviet spy ring and to indicate the dangers and weaknesses of the Soviet Espionage Service. It would have been easy to embellish the whole thing and produce a sensational document, but I have adhered to the truth. Where the laws of libel permit, and where I knew them, I have used real names. The press cuttings regarding my trial provide the only written evidence I have of the truth of the narrative. If any reader has an entree to the Swiss police archives he will find there an admirable dossier containing much regarding the activities of our organisation. Another easier proof could be provided if I cared to take a journey to Germany and walk into the Soviet Zone. This would perhaps provide only negative evidence, since I would never be heard of again, and it is a step I am reluctant to take at the moment. The condemned criminal seldom prefers to adjust the noose himself.

Condemned I certainly am. When I walked out of the Soviet Zone and gave up my career as a Russian spy I was as surely condemned to death by the Russians as any criminal by a black-capped judge and through the due processes of law. The Soviet system knows only one penalty for failure or treachery—death. My colleague Rado failed and is dead. I betrayed and as a result am equally condemned; and the sentence would be executed without mercy or delay were I ever to fall into Russian hands. History has shown the fate of other "traitors," like Krivitsky and Trotsky, who managed to get out and live at liberty for some time. A Russian wall at dawn or the death camps of the N.K.V.D. have seen many who did not achieve even that degree of freedom.

But to return to that flat in St. John's Wood. I pressed the bell and walked in.

2
So Easily You

"You will proceed to Geneva. There you will be contacted and further instructions will be given you." The voice of my vis-à-vis was quiet and matter-of-fact; and the whole atmosphere of the flat was one of complete middle-class respectability. Nothing could have been more incongruous than the contrast between this epitome of bourgeois smugness and the work that was transacted in its midst. Those seventeen words recruited me into the Red Army Intelligence. That I did not know at the time; nor did I even know exactly what I was expected to do. Indeed, looking round at the room, at those chintz-covered armchairs, those suburban lace curtains, it would have been more appropriate to imagine that I was being engaged as a Cook's courier. But before dealing with the events which succeeded my recruitment, a little background must be given. This will show the stages in the journey which led me to that London flat.

A psychoanalyst would be hard put to find anything in my early life which would indicate that one day I should be running a portion of a Soviet network. My upbringing was as ordinary as that of any child of middle-class parentage brought up between the wars. On leaving school I tried my hand at many jobs, ranging from managing a small business to running a garage, but never found anything which satisfied me for any length of time. I moved from job to job hoping that I would one day find something which suited me.

It is difficult for anyone, including myself, to look back dispassionately and objectively at those times and to try to analyse the feelings one had and the motives for one's actions. It was not really political sense or political education which shaped my decisions, leading me from the industrial Midlands to Switzerland, to postwar Russia, and ultimately back to England again. From a restless sales manager to a Russian spy is a difficult game of consequences and I can only hope that these pages will explain why and how, and the subsequent metamorphosis from a spy into a gentleman of leisure with much time to reflect and little to do.

However, it was almost inevitable that my early discontent and restlessness and desire for something new, preferably exciting, would lead me toward the Communist Party. While still in business I had attended Communist Party discussion groups and gradually was led to believe that international Communism was the panacea for all the world's ills. Others have travelled the same road—as the Royal Commission's report on the Canadian spy case shows—but at the time I had no idea as to where the road would end, and indeed, in all fairness to my fellow members, neither had they.

The outbreak of the Spanish Civil War crystallised my somewhat inchoate thoughts on the whole matter. Until that time I had been convinced that something was wrong but had found precise analysis difficult. The Civil War in Spain seemed to show everything up in neat black and white, and I was convinced that the Rebels were inspired and supported by the German-Italian Fascists with the idea of their gaining control first of the peninsula and ultimately of Europe and the entire world, with the resultant suppression of freedom and democratic thought. Ranged against these enemies of democracy were the Spanish Republican government, almost alone, with the Western democracies standing by, busily tying their own hands in the red tape of non-intervention. Rallying to their aid were only the freedom-loving individuals of the world and the Soviet Union. It all seemed as simple as that. I did not realise then that the Soviet Union, just as much as Germany and Italy, was using Spain as the European Salisbury Plain for trying out their own war machines, or that the freedom-loving individuals were to sacrifice their lives in thousands for some propagandist's whim or to gain a political battle desired by the politicos in Barcelona or some commissar from the Kremlin.

In those days Spanish affairs divided themselves into right and wrong for me as indeed I think they did for everyone. It was the bounden duty of anyone who valued democracy to do his best to support the existing government in Spain by whatever means he could. *I* had no other means than my two hands, and I was prepared to use them for the purpose. Many others felt the same way and travelled by the same road. Many did not return; they died in the dusty trenches round Madrid and Fuentes de Ebro.

Not till many years later was I told in Moscow that it had not been in the interests of the Soviet Union for the Republicans to win the Civil War. The Soviet policy was to provide only such a dribble of arms and ammunition as would keep the Republican forces in the field while allowing the Germans and Italians to install themselves firmly in the peninsula. The Russian idea was that any power which had a predominant influence in Spain was automatically the enemy of Great Britain, and the Russians desired to prevent any possible alliance between Britain and the Rome-Berlin Axis; which alliance the crystal-gazers in the Kremlin had deemed possible and which they regarded as fatal to Russian interests. This was Realpolitik with a vengeance but after years of working for the Russians I was not surprised when it was told to me. I think that had I been told this when in Spain I would have rejected it as so many Fascist lies. My comrades fell believing that they were fighting for freedom. In some ways their lot was enviable.

This preamble may seem dull, but so many books have been written about what a spy does and so few as to how he came to do it: and fewer still as to why he ever decided to become a spy. Both the operations of a spy and the method of his recruitment are matters which can be laid down in textbooks, whether English, German, or Russian. They are merely technical methods. The reasons for becoming a spy may range from greed through fear to patriotism or idealism, depending on whether the individual believes in a country or a cause. The average German spy who came to this country during the war was impelled by either greed or fear—fear of reprisals on his family—or both. The mercenary in any profession is not an attractive character—not even in espionage—and my German opposite numbers in the last war do not seem to have been actuated by any but the most mercenary of motives in most cases. I think I can say, speaking for myself and my colleagues, that the mercenary motive was subsidiary. Patriotism was obviously not applicable when one had English, German, Hungarian, and Swiss subjects all working for the same cause. Nor can it be said that in every case idealism was the primary cause. It was certainly not so in my case, since it was some time before I realised for whom I was working. Many conversations that I have had since with others who were "in the net" have shown that they, too, at first had little if any idea of the identity of their masters—save that their work was for the Communist ideal as a whole, which is, after all, the vaguest sort of master to have.

In my case I was recruited out of the dark into the dark—a sort of blind catch-as-catch-can—and went into the arena of international espionage with my eyes open, but under a black bandage. I knew that I was a spy and against whom I was supposed to be spying, but at first had no idea of the why and wherefore or of the directing hand. I wonder how many of my colleagues on the other side of the fence, who died in the early morning at Wandsworth Gaol, were in a similar position and died wondering.

3
IT ALL BEGAN IN SPAIN

It all really began in Spain. On a cold wet night in December 1936, I embarked for France. Most of my fellow volunteers were Party members, and most of them are dead. I myself, though not a Party member, had been vouched for by two responsible members of the Party, and as such departed to fight for my clear-cut ideals; to fight to prevent Fascism from overrunning Europe.

The journey into Spain was uneventful. We made our rendez-vous in Paris and were incorporated in a larger body of volunteers already collected there, and then sent on into Catalonia with responsible Party members as bear leaders. In Albacete, which was the headquarters of the International Brigade, we were all sorted out and I was posted to the nearby village of Madriguerras, where a British battalion was being formed.

Too many books have been written about the Spanish Civil War for me to say more than is necessary to my story. Too many of my comrades have died to make it easy for me to write about it at all. It was for me merely a halting place on my way. The fact that I did not realise that it was only a halting place and regarded it as the be-all and end-all of my existence at the time is neither here nor there. For me the war was a struggle where my friends fought and died. For others it was merely a testing ground and a suitable place for talent spotting.

The man in charge of the formation of the battalion was Wilfred Macartney. The political commissar was Douglas Springhall, who played a more vital part in my life later, when he recruited me for the Red Army Intelligence. Battalions were formed approximately on language groups and in our battalion we had British and dominion troops and a sprinkling of Swedes whose only other language was English. We even had an Ethiopian who claimed that he was the son of Ras Imru, one of the Negus' chieftains. After the preliminary flurry, however, it was discovered that he was merely a Lascar sailor who had picked up his English on British ships, and he then faded out of the propaganda limelight. Despite the occasional bad egg who is as inevitably attracted toward a cause where there is a possibility of loot as a fly is to honey, the morale of the battalion was high. Whatever were the motives of the Republican equivalents of brass hats, the rank and file fought magnificently. The casualty lists are sufficient evidence of this; almost half of the thousand-odd British who served with the International Brigade were killed.

I remember Professor J. B. S. Haldane, when for a short period he served with the brigade as a private soldier, standing in a trench, brandishing a tiny snub-nosed revolver, and shouting defiance at the advancing Franco infantry. Luckily for science, we managed to repel the Rebel attack and the professor was spared for his further contributions to world knowledge.

I was posted as battalion transport officer. Ranks at that time bore little relation to fact. I was not "politically reliable" and as such ranked lower in the political hierarchy than the fellow comrade who had sold the *Daily Worker* with distinction in North Shields. Though I never achieved commissioned rank, I performed all the duties for my battalion which would have been carried out in the British Army by a transport officer. The work was as varied as it was dangerous, ranging from the prosaic bringing up of the rations to the evacuation from an encircled town of the Republican *alcalde* with the entire civic funds. In this case the *alcalde* abandoned us first and fell promptly into the hands of skirmishing Moorish cavalry. The funds, however, lingered for days in the boot of the car, as we had rashly supposed that the mayor had been evacuating his wardrobe rather than his revenue. It was on such a trip, with Franco planes machine-gunning the road, that, bundling without dignity into a nearby shell hole, I was stepped softly on by Slater, then on the Planning Staff, who was similarly hurrying for shelter from the back seat of my car. He curled himself gracefully down on top of me with an exquisitely polite "Excuse me" which I have always treasured as a fine example of courtesy under difficulties.

There were not unnaturally preliminary teething pains in the battalion. One of these resulted in the Irish contingent's transferring in a body to the American Lincoln Battalion; they refused to serve under Macartney because he had been an officer in the Black and Tans in Ireland after World War I. Eventually the British Battalion was included in the 6th International Brigade, which for the greater part of the Civil War formed part of the 11th Division of the Republican Army.

This division was commanded by a Russian-trained General "Walter," who recently became Minister for War in the Polish government. By using his Christian name he was following the example of his Soviet colleagues, who preferred to veil their identities behind a noncommittal first name. I myself came into close touch with only one Red Army officer while in Spain; this was a certain "Max" who, despite his junior rank of captain and his function as "observer," wielded great authority. He came into my life again later when his endorsement of my suitability for work for the Red Army Intelligence helped to establish me in the confidence of the Russian D.M.I.

As an infantry soldier the strategy and politics of the war naturally passed me by. We, fighting in the line, knew little or nothing of Barcelona and Valencia politics and intrigues, and less still of their international ramifications. We only knew that we fought, always ill equipped and frequently underarmed, against an enemy who appeared to be furnished with a multiplicity of modern weapons. Our task was not made easier by the frequent "purges" of our officers which took place. After every reverse we could be certain that one or more of our colleagues would vanish—failure and "Trotskyist inclinations" being almost synonymous. Attacks did fail. This is hardly surprising when an army, often with only five live rounds a day to fire off, is thrown against a well-equipped force with modern weapons and stiffened with foreign troops. Not all our failures, however, can be attributed either to the Republican General Staff or to the lack of equipment. The "Moscow Operation" of Fuentes de Ebro will long be remembered by those who were lucky enough to survive it.

It appeared that Moscow had evolved a new tank theory which they wished tried out, not in mock combat but in battle conditions, which were found, conveniently and economically, in Spain. (I have no more bitterness toward the Russians for this technique than I have toward the Germans and the Italians, who did exactly the same thing. The only difference is that the Germans were publicly arraigned for it at Nuremberg.) The idea was to throw some forty tanks against the enemy during the siesta. These tanks were to break through the infantry front line and push straight forward to the artillery and, having disposed of the latter, turn back and take the infantry in the rear. The tanks were brand-new and the crews were Germans newly trained in a Russian tank school. It was in vain that our chief of staff, Malcolm Dunbar, pointed out that the rebel position had been heavily plastered with artillery fire, with the result that the irrigation ditches had been broken and the place was a quagmire. Moscow orders were orders, and the attack went in. Some twelve out of the forty tanks returned; the majority of the rest were captured intact by the enemy. I trust that the lesson was instructive to the Russian observers. It was certainly so to the surviving tank crews, who drove their Russian commander back to the base area never to be seen again.

This is, however, all past history, and the average person nowadays has forgotten the Civil War or remembers it merely as a curtain raiser to the second Great War. Of course it *was* such, and my comrades in their unmarked graves round Teruel were merely the first skirmishers in the great encounter to come.

After two years' continual service with the International Brigade, I was sent back on leave to England in September 1938 to be present at the Communist Party Congress at Birmingham. The political commissariat at the brigade must have regarded me with some favour to allow me, a non-Party member, to be selected to return. My job as transport officer made me less vulnerable to accusations as a "Trotskyist" and my personal friendship with my own particular commissar may have helped. I left the brigade, decimated by losses and beginning to be demoralised by "purges," never to return.

The original intention had been that I should return to Spain—though not as a fighting member of the I.B. The Party had decided that I was a suitable person to run a Red Cross truck which was to go to Spain from England at regular intervals, carrying medical supplies and comforts. This part of the assignment was highly respectable. The organisation which ran the service was non-Communist and the funds were raised by public subscription. This was to be only my "cover." My real job was to have been as a courier between King Street (the headquarters, then as now, of the British Communist Party) and the Communist command of the British Battalion of the brigade. I was also to have acted as a *passeur* for unauthorised persons who wished to enter Spain (it will be remembered that by this time non-intervention was in full swing and frontier control had been tightened up) and as a smuggler of unauthorised goods. I was also to ensure that the lion's share of the goods in my truck went to the politically enlightened. This job, however, fell through. To this day I do not know whether it in fact ever existed or whether it was merely put up to me to see my reactions to employment which was, to say the least, not quite what it seemed and definitely illegal Party work. Whether the offer was genuine or not does not really matter. The job was stillborn and that particular move in the undercover game of chess was over. It was Red's turn to move again and another pawn was put out temptingly. I accepted the move and the real game began.

After the Congress in Birmingham and a few days' leave, I returned to London and reported to King Street to discuss the Red Cross job. I was there met by Fred Copeman, who told me that the whole project had fallen through. Fred was an old friend, as he had been at one time commander of the British Battalion of the

I.B. He invited me to his flat in Lewisham for a meal with him and his wife. After supper the next move was made.

"Springhall has been asked to recommend someone for an assignment. We have discussed various people and think that you might fit the bill. I know nothing about the assignment save that it will be abroad and will be very dangerous."

I think that was all Fred Copeman did in fact know. He was in this case merely acting as the mouthpiece for Springhall. Though the latter remained in the background, his role as talent spotter and recruiter was clear. I always—and events have so far not proved me wrong—regarded him as the contact man for the Red Army in the British Communist Party. Gossip in Spain went so far as to state that he had held Red Army rank in his time. As far as his part in my recruitment went, I know no more than I have already stated. As any reader of the newspapers will remember, Springhall was later tried and convicted for a similar offence during the war. Fred Copeman's part in these preliminary flirtations was obscure. He was, I believe, merely on the fringe of the Soviet net and was used by Springhall and the others as an innocent cover for their contact work. Certainly my subsequent questioning of him seemed to show that he was as much in the dark as I was. Later, of course, Copeman split with the Party and joined the Oxford Group.

Despite the vagueness of the offer I jumped at it. Looking back on the whole affair in cold blood, it is a little difficult to understand why I should have accepted such an assignment with no notion whom I was working for or for what purpose. If someone had told me at the time that after six months at the work I should still have no idea as to the identity of my masters, I should have laughed at them. But such is in fact the case, and I think that many of those who were on the fringes of, for example, the Canadian case must have found themselves in a similar predicament.

However, I soon realised that the work for which I was destined was illegal, and very soon afterwards it became clear to me that I was ultimately intended for espionage work. It was soon apparent that I could not be working for the British Communist

Party. I thought that perhaps I was working for the German Communist Party (K.P.D.) or perhaps for the Comintern (as regards the inner workings of the latter I knew little more than did the average reader of the papers). But here I am slightly outrunning events. I may ultimately have been a good spy, but as regards my early career I was certainly an innocent abroad.

After my acceptance of the offer Copeman told me to go to an address in St. John's Wood. There I went one fine October morning and duly found myself inside the flat with the green door.

I have already related the instructions that I received there. They were not illuminating, and I learned nothing much more from the respectable housewife with a slight foreign accent who interviewed me. Her name I never knew for certain, though I have my own ideas on the subject. She was certainly friendly with, if not actually related to, my contact and spy master, or rather spy mistress, in Switzerland. Our business was done with briskness and despatch. I do not suppose that I was in the house more than ten minutes. I was dealt with by the lady of the house as briskly and impersonally as she would have engaged a housemaid.

Apart from the directions as to where I was to go, I also received a few further instructions to enable me to make contact with the person who was to deal with me in the future. I was to present myself outside the General Post Office in Geneva. (A favourite rendezvous, as a G.P.O. is easily found and provides an admirable excuse for loitering.) I was to be wearing a white scarf and to be holding in my right hand a leather belt. As the clock struck noon I would be approached by a woman carrying a string shopping bag containing a green parcel, and holding an orange in her hand. One would have thought that this would have been sufficient to enable anyone to contact anyone, even an unknown, in the middle of a Swiss street. But to avoid any possibility of error the whole rendezvous was made even more precise. The woman would ask me, in English, where I had bought the belt; and I was to reply that I had bought it in an ironmonger's shop in Paris. Then I was to ask her where I could buy an orange like hers, and she was to say that I could have hers for an English penny. Hardly sparkling dialogue,

but sufficient to ensure that the meeting was foolproof and an example of the usual thoroughness of my employers. For a similar
type of rendezvous I refer the reader to the details of the contact
which Professor Nunn May was to make with an unknown outside
the British Museum. The technique and indeed the choice of locale are exactly parallel.

I left this snug little St. John's Wood spy nest in some confusion of mind. I had no objection to the illegality and obviously clandestine nature of the mission which I had accepted. Looking back,
I do not think that espionage even entered my head at the time.
The average person does not think immediately of a spy mission
when he is offered a job, even when it is hedged round with such
Oppenheim secrecy as this one was. Nowadays I suppose that one
would merely think one had fallen in with a particularly well-
organised gang of black marketeers. At that time, if I *did* think, I
probably imagined that I had been cast for some Scarlet Pimper-
nel-like role of rescuing prisoners from Dachau. In fact I do not
believe that I thought at all. I was pleased enough to be offered a
job, and satisfied that since it came from the Party it would not
clash with my political opinions.

It was as neat a piece of recruiting as I met throughout my career with the Russians. Admittedly I was a small fish and an easy
one to hook and land at that; but the technique showed considerable experience. First the offer of the job which, though illegal,
was in fact straight Party work; then the change of assignment to
something quite unknown but obviously even more illegal. The fish
was well hooked and my employers could be certain that if I accepted a shot in the dark such as this Geneva appointment must
appear to a tyro, they could be equally sure that I would not balk
at anything further. Even if I did, what had they to lose? I could
have gone round to Scotland Yard with my story, and they would
be hardly a pennyworth the wiser. All I could have told them was
an address in St. John's Wood (which I afterward checked and
found to be one of impeccable, if foreign, respectability) and a confused story of a complicated rendezvous which in all probability
they would have put down to the maunderings of an unbalanced

individual with spy mania. It is certain that, had I blown the gaff, the rendezvous would have been cancelled and any special branch officer who had undertaken the long and tedious journey to Geneva would not have been rewarded by the sight of a woman laden with an orange.

Confusion of mind or no confusion of mind, I resolved to go on with the whole affair, and returned home to collect my kit and make the necessary arrangements for a visit to Switzerland. I had not much time, as the date of the rendezvous was only a few days ahead. Luckily in those days travel was easy and I soon found myself on the boat crossing the Channel. My last crossing had been on an equally clandestine mission—to fight for what I thought was freedom. Then I had my comrades with me. This time I was alone and moving into the dark.

A hardened spy regards a rendezvous with his contact as a matter of routine. If the contact is successful, so much the better. If it fails, then there are a variety of reasons which may have occasioned the failure, only a few of which may affect the personal safety or comfort of the spy himself. The human character is infinitely adaptable, and after a short time I regarded clandestine meetings and undercover assignments as the normal course of duty. It would be idle to pretend, however, that I went to this, my first assignment, with complete sangfroid. My attitude of mind was similar to that of the debutante at her first dance: extreme nervousness with a lively anticipation of pleasure and excitement to come.

Geneva is not an exciting town. The centre for international espionage in two wars, it singularly fails to come up to expectations. Swiss architecture, admirable as it may be, does not supply that Ruritanian atmosphere of the dark alley and the shuttered casement which should go with the meeting of agents. It may be for this reason that it is such a favourite for clandestine encounters. A meeting of the Inquisition with Torquemada in the chair would there take on the semblance of normality of a parochial council. It must be remembered also that at that time the dove of League peace was still hovering over the town. Slightly bedraggled after Munich, she was still surrounded with an aura of international amity, as bogus, alas, as my role of tourist. It would be difficult to have found a more cynical rendezvous for a spy meeting. Nor is it really relevant that I was only one of many members of varied and various spy rings who were hurrying there for meetings of varying degrees of secrecy and respectability.

Remaining true to my role as a tourist, I stayed at a small hotel near the station and on the appointed day went to the post office for the rendezvous, armed with the necessary paraphernalia for my contact. Anyone who has ever attempted to pick someone up under the clock at Charing Cross station, with the usual marks of identification dear to the writers of notices in the personals column of the *Times*, can imagine my feelings. It seemed that all the hausfraus of Geneva had conceived the happy idea of supplying their loved ones with a nice orange for their midday meal and all Geneva wrapping paper appeared green. All the women looked equally respectable and equally indifferent. Holding my leather strap, I felt a self-conscious fool and an ass, at best self-doomed to embarrassment and at worst to a Swiss charge of accosting.

The local clocks announced, rather smugly to my heated imagination, that noon had arrived, and not one of the crowd swirling past the steps had even vouchsafed me a glance. Then I noticed her. Punctuality may be the politeness of princes but it is certainly a perquisite of Soviet spies. Slim, with a good figure and even better legs, her black hair demurely dressed, she stood out from the Swiss crowd. In her early thirties, she might have been the wife of a minor French consular official. Her bag contained a green parcel and she held an orange.

"Excuse me, but where did you buy that belt?"

Contact had been established.

4
AN INNOCENT ABROAD

Seldom if ever can a spy have gone on a mission with so few technical qualifications and knowledge as I. Speaking only inferior French, a little kitchen Spanish, and elementary German, I was not exactly qualified for work on the Continent. Knowing nothing of wireless or other secret means of communication, I was equally ill equipped to communicate any information that I might acquire; and I laboured under the additional handicap of not knowing for whom I was working. My only qualifications were my native common sense, a capacity to judge a position and sum up a situation correctly and succinctly, and, most important in Russian eyes, a good political background. That I ended my career as a spy speaking fluent French and passable German, an efficient wireless operator capable of building my own set, and with a working knowledge of microphotography and the simpler secret inks, speaks, I think, more highly for my adaptability than for the efficiency of the Russian Intelligence Service. In obtaining these qualifications I received no help and little encouragement from my masters. No one could have been more of an innocent in espionage than I was at first, and the fact that I lasted was more a matter of personal good luck than good judgment by the Russians. It must be remembered, however, that I was a "new boy" recruited *ad hoc* and for a network still in embryo. Their other networks were longer established and better installed. I should know, as in the end I was running one.

After having established contact, my new acquaintance and I adjourned prosaically for coffee. A pleasant person and an amusing companion, my first espionage contact was not as frightening as I had expected. She told me that she was unfortunately not allowed to reveal her name nor to tell me for whom I would be working—for the moment. I could call her Sonia. She spoke English with a slight foreign accent and was, I should judge, a Russian or a Pole—certainly a Slav. When I was finally established in the network I learnt her name. She was Maria Schultz and had had a long career as a Red agent. She and her husband, Alfred Schultz, had worked for the Red Army in Poland and the Far East. Her husband was, I gathered, still in the Far East and I believe at that time was under arrest by the Chinese for espionage activities. She was now starting up a network in Switzerland for work against Germany, and I was one of the first of her recruits. But all this I learnt later, and the only new knowledge that I had acquired in the café was her cover name—which for ease and clarity I shall continue to use throughout the narrative.

Sonia and I continued to meet for several days at various public rendezvous in Geneva, but I learnt little more of any interest. All I was told was that it had been decided that I was to go to Munich. There I was to install myself as a tourist and learn the language, make as many friends as possible, and keep my eyes open. Not very onerous or indeed explicit instructions, but after the Spanish front line it was a relief to know that the task described to me in London as "difficult and dangerous" was to be, at any rate for a start, so easy and pleasant. Sonia gave me two thousand Swiss francs for my expenses in Munich and fixed up a rendezvous in three months' time. This time it was to be in Lausanne but at the same locale, the General Post Office, and a series of hours and days were fixed in case anything went wrong.

It was with a light heart that I returned to England to collect my kit and get my visa. Early in November I arrived in Munich.

Munich at that time was a pleasant place. At least for an innocent abroad with enough pocket money and little to do save prepare political reports on Germany and for the rest of the time enjoy myself. I managed to pick up a fair circle of acquaintances and the only brainwork I attempted was to learn German—which I was taught by a local member of the S.S. who lived in the same pension. Time passed swiftly and pleasantly enough till my next rendezvous with Sonia in February.

The only happening of even remote interest during my first Munich stay was that I lit by accident on Hitler's *Stammtisch*. Looking one day for a cheap place to lunch, I happened on the Osteria Bavaria and, having settled down to the good 1/6d set lunch, I noticed a flurry at the door and Hitler strode in accompanied by his adjutant Bruecker, his photographer and toady Hoffmann, and two A.D.C.s. I discovered that the proprietor of the restaurant had been a fellow comrade during the first war; Hitler had lunched there on and off for over fifteen years and even now that he had reached power he ate there whenever he was in Munich. This I confirmed, as I made a habit of lunching there and saw him sometimes as often as three times a week. I mention this triviality as it was to have somewhat surprising consequences later.

My second contact with Sonia went off as smoothly as the first, and this time we had several quite long and moderately enlightening talks. It was during this visit that I learnt for the first time that my masters were the Red Army Intelligence. Sonia told me that she was engaged in setting up a new network for them in Switzerland and that my credentials had been referred back to the Russian D.M.I., who had made the necessary checkups, and that I was now on the strength as a "collaborator" at a salary of U.S. $150 a month and all reasonable expenses.

It is perhaps worth noting in passing that all Russian spy payments and accounts are made and calculated in United States dollars. The Red Army net had the strongest objections to dealing in any other sort of currency and went to endless trouble to secure dollars for payment.

Sonia said that in normal times I would have been sent to a special school in Moscow for at least a year on recruitment. There I would have been taught all the tricks of the trade such as W/T transmission, microphotography, secret inks, sabotage instruction, etc. As it was thought that an international crisis was imminent,

Moscow had decided to dispense with this in my case and I was to
return to Germany at once and study all these and kindred subjects on my own account.

Sonia gave me a cover name, Jim, and some idea of the elements of the game, especially in the matter of contacting my superiors or others in case of emergency. If I lost contact with her I
was to attempt to get into touch with the M.I. Directorate in Moscow through a Soviet military attaché. I was to go to the Soviet
M.A. in any country other than the one in which I was working or
of which I was a native. In my case, of course, this ruled out Berlin
and London. I was to use any device or artifice that I could think
of to get into the presence of the attaché himself and get him alone,
even to the extent of threatening any minor official with punish-
ment by the N.K.V.D. I was also expressly forbidden to mention
my name or show my passport to any official at the embassy—even
the attaché on my first visit. Having reached the presence, I was to
hand him a message for transmission to Moscow. In my case this
would run approximately as follows: "Jim operating in Jersey and
a native of Brazil has lost contact with Sonia who lives in Sicily
where she has a musical box and wishes to re-establish communication with the director." In other words "Foote operating in Germany and a native of Britain has lost contact with Maria Schultz
who lives in Switzerland where she has a wireless transmitter and
wishes to re-establish contact with the D.M.I." Only when the
attaché had received a reply giving the necessary instructions and
receiving permission from the D.M.I. to ask for my identity was I
allowed to disclose my name.

If for some reason I was unable to establish contact with a Soviet military attaché and the need was urgent (and funds permitted), I should take a ticket for the Far East via the Trans-Siberian
Railway and while in Moscow call at the headquarters of the Red
Army, which would put me in touch with the department concerned. Only in a last resort was I to go to Russia on an Intourist
ticket. Soviet agents were not allowed to keep passports which contained Intourist visas, as these might indicate to the outside world
that the holder was favourably inclined toward the regime. In such

cases the passport was taken away and a special department of the Soviet Intelligence removed the offending pages. This was a lengthy process and so this course was discouraged.

I was also told that later on I should be given a "place of conspiracy" which would be a fixed spot in some nearby country—probably Belgium or Holland. Certain fixed days and hours would be given me for contact and I would be told my own passwords and distinctive objects and also of course those of the contact. I was, however, to go there only if I lost contact with my group leader, Sonia, or on orders from the director.

All these arrangements sound slightly academic in the light of subsequent events. Cooped up in Switzerland, surrounded by countries at war with my own and later at war with Soviet Russia, the chances of meeting a Soviet attaché or of obtaining an Intourist visa were slight. As for places of conspiracy, these would have to be confined to Switzerland itself. In point of fact the emergency, luckily, never arose, as from the time that we were surrounded until the day of my arrest we always had at least two wireless sets working to Moscow at any one time.

While still in Lausanne, Sonia asked me to write out a report on political and economic conditions in Germany. She had also shown great interest in Hitler and my little Munich restaurant— which I had mentioned to her in the course of casual conversation. She sent my report back over her secret transmitter to the director and must have sent a separate report on the Hitler episode as I was told that the director was extremely interested in the report on Hitler and instructed me to check up on his movements and habits as well as I could.

Sonia also told me that I might expect to receive a visit from a new collaborator who would contact me in Munich and with whom I should have to operate in future. She added that it was possible that we would be asked to carry out some act of sabotage, the actual occurrence of which the director could check from his study of the press. I (and I gathered that this was a general instruction to all agents) was therefore to plan a possible sabotage operation and keep it, as it were, on ice until such time as the director

authorised it. Such a scheme could perform no really useful function except that of checking the reliability of an agent and his planning ingenuity, as it was unlikely that even the most fanatical Red
agent would put his head in the noose by some really profitable
sabotage scheme when he could much more easily and quietly
undertake some small-scale arson which would duly appear in the
local press and satisfy Moscow.

I returned to Germany after my short and this time moderately
constructive trip. I at least knew now for whom I was working, even
if the precise details of what I was supposed to do were still lack-
ing. I was not unnaturally curious as to the identity of the "collaborator" whom I had been promised. I could only hope that he
might be somewhat more versed in the technique of espionage than
I was. In this respect I was to be sadly disappointed. I do not know
whether the reader has suffered from the same nightmare that I
used to have as a child. I would dream that I was about to conduct
a symphony orchestra and the whole audience was assembled,
ready and waiting, and the orchestra poised for the first tap of my
baton. At that moment I would suddenly realise that not only did I
not know the piece which I was supposed to conduct but also that
I was unable to read a note of music. On such occasions in dreams,
one merely wakes up in a cold sweat. In real life, working for the
Russians, it happened only too often—and there was no awaken-
ing.

Before I left Sonia gave me U.S. $900 ($450 for three months'
salary and a similar sum for three months' expenses). My instructions were not varied. Indeed variations on such a vague theme
were hardly possible. I continued to lunch at the Osteria and observe the Fuehrer at such times as he visited the place, and otherwise maintained my previous contacts and continued to learn German. The place was, of course, still full of tourists basking in the
twilight of European peace. English and American, they still continued to flock to Munich to observe the picturesqueness of the
past and the preparations for the future. The former they found
more interesting. Van Gogh had not yet been banished from the

Neue Pinakothek and only the memorial to the fallen of the Munich
Putsch really marked the New Germany. The shadow of the Cham-
berlain umbrella still lay heavy over the political scene. Anyone
who delved deeper could see how thin this veneer of peace really
was. Conversations with my S.S. friends and the evidence of my
eyes convinced me that it was only a matter of time before the military machine took control and the country went to war. I felt sure
that when this happened England would be involved and consequently anything that I could do then or later against Germany
would be of value. The future position of Russia was then, as always, enigmatic. There were rumours going about Munich of a
possible German-Russian rapprochement but these did not seem
to tally with the oft-repeated tirades of Nazi leaders against the
Bolshevik Menace and the Red Terror. In the interval before the
storm burst I was prepared to go on with the tasks given me by
Sonia. The future could take care of itself—and the future did.

In April I received the expected call from my "collaborator." It
was an unexpected call from an old friend. The doorbell of my pension in Elizabeth Strasse rang, and the maid ushered in a colleague
whom I had not seen since the days of the Spanish War. I was as-
tounded that he had found me, as I had, on instructions, severed
all connections with the brigade and even my own family did not
know that I was in Germany. I soon discovered that this was no
social call but that he was in fact my new fellow worker in Sonia's
network in Germany.

Bill Philips (or, to give him his Soviet cover name, Jack) had
been recruited in exactly the same way as I. In fact I had been indirectly responsible for his recruitment, as I had given King Street
his name as a likely candidate to succeed me in the job of courier
to Spain. He had worked with me in brigade transport in Spain
and, quite apart from our jobs being side by side, we had been
drawn together as he was not a Party member either. (It is not without significance that, as far as Sonia was concerned, the network
that she set up consisted of almost entirely non-Party members—
though their anti-Fascist records were impressive. This was, after
all, mere common sense on the part of Moscow. A Party member

32   ALEXANDER FOOTE

would be *ipso facto* suspect. It would take quite a lot of foreign
police digging to discover my past—open as it was.)

Bill had already set himself up in Frankfurt, having received
instructions as vague and unsatisfactory as mine. He had been told
specifically only that he was to keep an eye on the I. G. Farben
factory and to help me in the "Hitler scheme."

It was news to me that this was in fact a scheme. At our last
meeting Sonia had told me to keep a general eye on Hitler's movements, but in the subsequent two months the idea had burgeoned
in the eyes of the Kremlin into a full-blown scheme for assassination with Bill and me apparently cast for the principal roles. We
were neither of us very willing actors as neither of us really fan-
cied a martyr's crown—especially since on the face of it the scheme
appeared suicidal and doomed to failure. We did feel, however,
that in fairness to our employers, who, after all, had been paying
us for some months with little or no return for their money, it be-
hooved us to look into the matter—and the result was not unprom-
ising.

It was not necessary to reconnoitre the field because I knew
the restaurant extremely well. Hitler always lunched in a private
room which was separated only by a thin wooden partition from
the corridor leading from the restaurant to the lavatories. It was
along this partition that the coats of the customers were hung. As
far as we could gather there was no special surveillance of the place
and no extra precautions were put into force when the Fuehrer
honoured it with his presence. What could be easier, we argued,
than to put a time bomb in an attaché case along with our coats
and, having had an early lunch, abandon the lot in the hope that
the bomb would blow Hitler and his entourage, snugly lunching
behind the deal boarding, into eternity. Looking back on the
scheme now, it appears to me to have been well-nigh foolproof. It
also bears a startling resemblance to the July 1944 attempt by
Stauffenberg. In his case wooden partitions caused the scheme to
fail: the blast escaped and Hitler survived. We were too innocent
then to know of the niceties of explosives, but as the other three
walls were solid Bavarian stone it seems likely that we might have

been successful. But the whole affair never got further than the planning stage. It is easy enough as an officer cadet to plan a Tactical Exercise without Troops. It is equally easy as a cadet spy to plan a Sabotage Exercise without Explosives. In both cases the individual has the power and not the ultimate responsibility. The officer cadet will blithely throw away a company in a dashing assault on an impregnable position, knowing that the worst that can befall him is a low mark. Similarly we planned the operation knowing that the worst that could befall us would be a sour look from Sonia.

Determined, however, to earn our keep, on paper if not in practice, we went even further and planned an alternative scheme which involved assassination in its more traditional character—by revolver rather than T.N.T. It was Hitler's habit to proceed down the restaurant en route to his private room, acknowledging the plaudits of the lunchers who, not unnaturally, rose to their feet on the entrance of the head of the state. One day Bill stationed himself at the table next to the gangway, and as Hitler approached put his hand rapidly and furtively into his pocket—and drew out a cigarette case. I on the other side of the room watched the reactions of Hitler's entourage and the rest of the lunchers—among whom one imagined there must have been a fair sprinkling of trigger-happy Gestapo agents. Nothing whatever happened. No reaction was visible—though to my heated imagination no action could have looked more suspicious. Looking back on this, it all seems incredibly jejune—even though Bill's act required a considerable amount of personal courage as, if the guards had been alert, it would have been small comfort to him to have been beaten to the draw—of a cigarette.

With such innocent sports Bill and I whiled away our time in Munich together. He had little more to do in Frankfurt than I had in Munich, and preferred to come down and see me so that we could do nothing together.

In May I met Sonia again at Vevey at the end of the three months' period. She urged me to go on with further plans for the Hitler assassination plot. I agreed to look into the matter in greater detail, which I had no intention whatsoever of doing. There was no more planning to be done—all that was necessary was an explosive suitcase or a potential suicide—and Sonia's network could provide neither. I returned to a Germany where such plots were still only in the backs of the minds of German generals.

There was one more sabotage exercise during our German period. This scheme was born of Bill's enthusiasm for his job. He had discovered that there was a Zeppelin in a hangar close to Frankfurt and conceived the brilliant notion of burning it up. I never saw it, and Bill's description was confused, but I have always imagined that it was the Graf Zeppelin, which was frequently paraded round Germany on show. Bill said that it would be perfectly easy to put a time bomb with a slow fuse in a cigarette packet under one of the seats and let it and the hydrogen in the envelope do the rest. The next step was of course the manufacture of an incendiary mixture. Sonia had given me instructions in the compounding of an efficient incendiary mixture from chemicals which could be bought easily and openly. After this lapse of time I am vague as to the formula but remember that sugar, aluminum powder, and charcoal were among the ingredients. A moderately accurate time fuse was not difficult to make with two chemicals separated by a division which would be dissolved by acid action in a specified length of time depending on the thickness of the partition. Bill and I conducted simple but satisfactory experiments in a secluded meadow near Munich. However, I was not at all convinced that it would set fire to the leather cushion of the seat in the Zeppelin under which it would have to be concealed. I was also under the impression, I believe now wrongly, that they used a helium rather than a hydrogen filling for the envelope with the result that we would have to rely on the combustion of the interior fittings alone with no assistance from the gas in the envelope. Before I could go further with my experiments I was summoned to Vevey to an emergency meeting with Sonia. This was in August and coincided with Bill's routine visit at the end of his three months' period.

Sonia was extremely excited over the scheme—even more so than she had been over the Hitler plot. We discussed the whole thing at length, walking up and down the front at Vevey. Sonia was convinced that it would work. I was equally certain that the whole thing would be a flop from the start and that even if the bomb could be planted unobserved the incendiary mixture would ignite nothing save itself.

Ultimately Sonia invited me back to her home so that we could try out the mixture in peace and quiet. This was the first time that I had been asked to her house. Previously we had always met at agreed rendezvous, and I felt that it was a step forward in my initiation into the network. Sonia lived in a modest little chalet at Caux sur Montreux with her two children and her old German nurse. As pretty a domestic, bourgeois atmosphere as one could find anywhere. The only slightly incongruous note was struck by the two bits of her wireless transmitter, which at that time, with incredible carelessness, she used to leave lying about the house. Not at all the setup one would expect for a Russian agent of long standing.

After dinner we adjourned to the loggia to test out the bomb. We placed the mixture underneath one of Sonia's sofa cushions which she sacrificed for the purpose. As I had thought, the only result was a large quantity of black smoke and an unholy stink. By mutual agreement no further mention was made of the Zeppelin scheme.

But while we had been indulging in amateur pyrotechnics, fireworks on a larger and more European scheme began to go off. About August 23 I was ordered to return to my post in Munich. I boarded the train for Germany in Lausanne but almost before I had settled down and before the train was fairly under way, to my astonishment Sonia entered the carriage and sat down opposite. Luckily the only other occupant left for a few moments and in a hurried whisper Sonia told me that she felt certain that Great Britain would fight and that despite Moscow's orders it would be better for me to delay my return until things became a little clearer one way or the other. We arranged a series of rendezvous on alternate days in Berne, and I left the train and returned to Montreux.

I was not unnaturally somewhat concerned over Bill, who had returned to Germany and was taking a holiday at Titisee on his way back to his post at Frankfurt. Sonia, on the other hand, refused to be perturbed, saying that Moscow would send orders in good time and that for the moment he could do no harm: an attitude not really consistent with her concern over my return to Munich. Sonia was, however, oversanguine as to the solicitude of the Kremlin for their minor operatives in potentially enemy countries. The German-Russian pact hit us like a thunderbolt out of a clear sky. Such a volte-face had never been regarded as practical politics by most people and such rumours of German-Russian flirtations as had reached Switzerland were in the main regarded as merely journalist bar gossip. The first and only reaction to the pact that we had from Moscow was a day later when Sonia received a message to pull all the agents she could out of Germany and break all contact with any remaining resident agents.

This was my first experience of Russian Realpolitik and it came as something of a shock. Its effect on Sonia, who was an old guard Communist and had for the past eight years regarded Fascism as the major world menace, was of course shattering. As a good Party member she had had Party discipline drilled into her until it was second nature for her to obey the whims of a Party directive—but she had always regarded the main Party line as being firmly and steadfastly directed against Fascism. At one blow all this was changed and she, as a good Party member, had now to regard the Nazis as her friends and the democracies as her potential foes. Such a *bouleversement* of all her preconceived ideas was really too much for her. Working as an undercover agent, she had naturally been less subjected to Party propaganda at first hand than her more docile colleagues, who obeyed the behest of King Street—or rather of Moscow relayed through King Street. The latter obediently trimmed their sails to the prevailing wind from the steppes. Sonia, too, paid lip service to her orders and obediently disbanded the organisation that she had been at such pains to build up; but I think that from that time onward her heart was not in the work. She continued to obey such orders as she received and carried out operations to the best of her ability, but at the first opportunity she pulled out and returned to England. In a way she was lucky to have received her disillusionment early in the war. She had worked for many years for what she thought was a righteous cause, and she was spared the final discovery that that cause was not an idealistic crusade but merely power politics in its crudest form.

While Sonia was wrestling with her political conscience I was left with the more practical difficulty of recalling Bill from Germany. As anyone who has tried knows, continental telephoning at the best of times is a game which requires patience and an equable temper. Transfrontier telephoning provides an additional hazard. Add to both these an imminent European war and a plethora of nervous switch censors at the main exchanges on both sides of the border, and it ceases to become a game of skill and degenerates into a haphazard game of chance. In this case I was lucky and after the waste of only several valuable hours, an uncounted number of francs, and the last remnants of what had once been a placid temperament, I managed to get through to Bill where he was sun-bathing beside the lake and told him to get out of Germany as fast as he could. He appeared somewhat surprised, as international events had apparently by-passed his rural retreat and certainly gone over his head. He managed to get out to Switzerland with a few hours to spare. We waited to see what the world and Moscow would next bring forth. The former brought us war soon enough. As for the latter, Moscow evidently decided that discretion was the best course and during the first week of a Europe at war we received no kind of instruction. Heaven knows we had done little enough for the past year, but it was somewhat galling to think that the little we had done was apparently to be completely wasted. I need not have bothered. There would be work enough before I found rest in a Swiss prison.

5

Swiss Interlude

My career as a resident Russian agent in Switzerland divides itself roughly into two parts. The first, while I was still working with Sonia, covers the period of the phony war; the second lasted roughly from the time of Sonia's departure in December 1940 to my arrest by the Swiss in November 1943. The latter period was the more strenuous, and during it I used to look back wistfully on the pleasant pastoral interlude while the war was still static and Switzerland, as an intelligence centre, moderately stagnant.

The first message that Sonia received after the outbreak of war instructed us to remain quietly in Switzerland and ordered Bill and me to learn short-wave transmission.

The autumn and winter of 1939 passed peacefully enough for us all. No further instructions were received and Sofia used her transmitter only for the despatch of periodic economic and political reports which were more in the nature of sops to Moscow.

Bill and I settled down quietly in a small pension in Montreux and used to proceed periodically up the hill for elementary instruction in wireless transmission given us by Sonia. We also did our best to gain some kind of a clue as to wireless construction. A few beginners' textbooks and some hints from Sonia were all the help we got, but by the end of the winter I was a moderately proficient operator and had some idea as to radio construction, and Bill was in a fair way to becoming a useful operator.

As I said, Moscow worried us little during this period, and Sonia maintained contact only about once a month for the purpose of sending over her surveys. Moscow was leaving us severely alone. Our usefulness to them was past for the moment and the Red Army was content to allow the network to remain fallow until the time should come to revive it. Moscow, however, did produce one suggestion, which was that the whole network should move to Rumania. As it happened, I had made contact in Switzerland with a Rumanian diplomat and on Moscow's suggestion I explored the matter of visas and passports further; and in the end I did manage to work out a scheme by which Bill and I and Sonia and her entourage could move to Bucharest in comparative comfort and with our papers in almost legal order. The whole scheme fell through in the end, since it called for a certain amount of money to oil the machinery of the Rumanian passport office. Moscow was beginning to feel the pinch and dollars were not quite so readily forthcoming in Switzerland as they had been in the past. Looking back on it now, I can only breathe a thankful sigh of relief that the scheme did not reach maturity, as Bill's and my positions in Bucharest a year or so later would have been, to say the least, ambiguous; and I cannot believe that Sonia's documentation would have stood up to a Gestapo scrutiny. The wife of a German, who himself was incarcerated in a Chinese jail for Communist activities, would hardly have been *persona grata* with the German authorities who were shortly to take over Rumania. On the whole it was perhaps better that we all remained quietly in neutral Switzerland, even though Moscow had clipped our espionage wings.

Moscow did, however, make life quite complicated for Sonia for a period, and caused her to take a little more care as to her cover and her activities. Just before the outbreak of war the Red Army had sent her a new recruit in the shape of "Alex." Alex was in fact a German who had fought in the International Brigade and had been sent to Sonia to set up another secret wireless set in Switzerland, which was to work as subordinate to Sonia's and also as a stopgap in case her set broke down or was seized. Had Sonia been allowed to continue to run her network into Germany the second set would have proved useful to carry the overflow of traffic which time would not allow her to carry on her set and in her schedules.

It would also have proved invaluable to me later when I was passing the majority of the traffic out of Switzerland, since it would have enabled me to remain for a shorter time on the air with my own set. As it was, I had to transmit almost throughout the night, a procedure which was asking for trouble from the Swiss police and the German monitoring.

Moscow, however, had been rather too ingenious, and Alex (Franz Ahlmann) proved in the end far more of a liability than an asset. He had been sent to us on a Finnish passport allegedly issued in Canada. His documentation as such was perfect, and on paper he could pass anywhere and indeed he arrived from Moscow via France without question. Unfortunately Alex could speak neither English nor Finnish, with one of which languages he must have had at least a bowing acquaintance had his papers been genuine. This the Swiss police were not slow in discovering. That in itself would not have been damaging, but unfortunately they raided his room when he was out and discovered in it a large quantity of wireless parts with which he was in the process of making a new transmitter. That also might have been laughed off as overenthusiasm by an amateur wireless enthusiast—but unfortunately he had been at Sonia's once when the police called on a routine checkup.

Subsequent events showed that the Swiss in this case were singularly obtuse or singularly kind and did not connect the litter of wireless parts in Alex's apartment with the quiet little villa at Caux. One reason was that the police officer in charge of the case had been blown up by an infernal machine which, in the course of his duties, he was attempting to immobilise. The affair caused some stir at the time as it was one of the earliest outward manifestations of the silent espionage war which was to rage in Switzerland for the next six years. We never knew whose bomb it was.

The whole affair shook Sonia severely and she thenceforth kept her transmitter buried in the garden—except for the times when it was actually in use. This increased the security of operations immeasurably (as opposed to the earlier, careless days when the whole thing was strewn about the house) but added equally greatly to the difficulty of working. For anyone who wishes to indulge in espionage, I do not recommend digging in a flower bed for a biscuit tin containing the essential bits of a transmitter with the scheduled time for a transmission fast approaching. It may be romantic and in the best tradition, but it is also exceedingly difficult and rather humiliating. Sonia's tulip bed was not improved, and the set developed the faults that might be expected to result from prolonged interment. We were not altogether pleased with the arrival of Alex and felt that the troubles he brought in his wake, which were not really his fault but resulted from the overenthusiasm of Moscow, greatly outweighed his potential value. Alex was to remain a headache for me throughout my stay in Switzerland. The Swiss were kind to him, and though they may have had a shrewd idea as to his potential activities they merely interned him as a foreigner whose papers were out of order, and he was put on forced labour for the rest of the war. His position was not unpleasant as he had a certain amount of freedom and I was able to help him in a variety of ways. He was a perpetual drain on the rather limited finances of our organisation because Moscow ordered that he was to be kept in comfort. He passed a pleasant if slightly tedious war.

The only task Moscow gave us at this time was to send a courier from Switzerland to contact the wife and family of Thaelmann, the German Communist leader, who had been imprisoned by the Nazis. For this task Sonia sent her aged maid, Lisa Brockel, who managed to get an *aller et retour* visa without difficulty. After a certain amount of trouble she contacted Thaelmann's wife, who stated that Thaelmann himself was in Hamburg prison and, considering all things, fairly comfortable. The maid was not fully in the picture regarding Sonia's espionage activities, but as she had been with the family for years and was devoted to Alfred Schultz, she obviously had a pretty shrewd idea as to what was going on. It was indeed her devotion to Schultz himself which caused the next crisis in our lives and nearly led to disaster.

Sonia was increasingly dissatisfied with the life and work and wished to return to England. The main obstacle, apart from Moscow's views, was of course her German passport. Therefore, in order to get British nationality, she managed to persuade Bill to agree to marry her if she could get a divorce from Schultz. She managed to obtain a divorce in the Swiss courts early in 1940, and straight away married Bill and was thus entitled to a British passport. This whole scheme was explained to Lisa, who was extremely distressed at this apparent disloyalty to her master. Sonia explained that the marriage was to be in name alone and that she had no intention of being unfaithful to Schultz but was merely adding one more to the numerous *mariages blancs* which were taking place in Switzerland at the time purely for the purpose of acquiring legal papers.

All would have been well had the scheme gone as planned, but there was another factor which had not been considered. Bill and Sonia fell deeply in love, and it was perfectly obvious that this was anything but a *mariage de convenance*. This disloyalty to Alfred's memory was more than Lisa could bear and she resolved to end it by desperate means. She thereupon rang up the British Consulate and denounced Sonia and Bill as Soviet spies and told them where the transmitter was hidden. As luck would have it, her English was so bad that no one at the consulate could understand what she was saying, and she was cut off by a bored clerk who merely added her name to the list of lunatics who pestered the consulate daily. It was perfectly obvious that as long as she remained in Switzerland— or Sonia and Bill remained in love—she would be a perpetual danger to us all. After endless argument she consented to return to her home in Germany. She was a faithful old thing and I was fond of and sorry for her. Had sex not reared its ugly head she would have been with us to the end, but it was too dangerous to have a weak link in the chain. It was bad enough to have the head of the network and your fellow operative acting like a honeymoon couple, without the thought that at any moment the faithful retainer might try yet another denunciation—and perhaps with more success.

Meanwhile the blitzkrieg had started and soon, with the fall of France, we in Switzerland were virtually isolated. The debacle in France had another and more immediate effect on the lives of us all, for at last we came into touch with espionage proper. The network into which we were now to be incorporated was the permanent Red Army organisation and had been in existence for years.

With headquarters in Switzerland, it operated throughout western Europe. Its ramifications and sources made Sonia's own independent organisation appear a trifle futile. In fairness to the latter, one must add that it had never really been given a chance, since, just as it was about to go into production, the Russo-German pact came into force and the whole enterprise was stillborn. Not so the permanent organisation (of which Sonia had no knowledge till Moscow told her); throughout the period of the phony war it had been building up its resources and agents and was never in any doubt as to its ultimate target—Germany. I gathered, in the course of my long association with the network, that originally part of its effort had been directed against Great Britain but that the rapidly growing danger of Nazi Germany occasioned a switch of its efforts and priorities some years before the outbreak of war. Certainly all the time that I was associated with it there was never any sign that its ramifications extended into England. This of course does not mean that there was no organisation working against England. Many indications show that there was, even if for political reasons it was lying dormant. If an old and trusted Russian spy like Sonia was in ignorance of a parallel organisation run by the same masters in the same country it was unlikely that we would learn of other ramifications into other countries—unless we had to—and the contingency never arose.

6

Sicilian Musical Box

It is now time to mention how we came into touch with the other "musical box" working in "Sicily" (to use the Russian cover names for the wireless sets working in Switzerland for the Red Army), and after that it will be necessary to give a picture of how the whole network was organised and what it achieved.

The reason the Russians were forced to put two independent organisations in touch with each other—a thing which every well-run espionage organisation dislikes intensely, as it naturally doubles the risk of compromise—was the unexpected success of the Germans in France, which led to a complete breakdown of communications.

The permanent Red Army net had in the past communicated its information by means of microphotographs which were taken by courier to Paris and thence forwarded to Moscow over a transmitter belonging to the subsidiary French network. The fall of Paris cut off this route, and the organisation was left in the air. As a result Sonia received orders to get into touch with "Albert," the head of the Red Army network in Switzerland, and place her transmitter at his disposal. Albert had in fact been told to construct a transmitter and train operators against just such a contingency—but had taken no action and was thus cut off from the "Centre" (as Moscow was known in the local jargon).

Albert was stationed in Geneva and Sonia went off to contact him and fix up communication arrangements. Albert was, in fact, Alexander Rado, a Hungarian cartographer and a Soviet agent of long standing. His position in Switzerland was impeccable; in this case Moscow had done their work well, as he was a partner in a Swiss firm of cartographers of great respectability and long standing. Very short and fat and speaking six languages fluently, he was himself an expert cartographer and used to prepare the war maps which appeared in all the Swiss papers. His wife, "Mary," was also "in the net" and in some ways the more dominant of the two in their partnership. Rado, as will be seen, lost his nerve in the end, but Mary was never affected, and I think that it was her influence that prevented Rado from breaking down earlier.

At first Sonia used to go to Geneva and collect Rado's enciphered traffic at an agreed rendezvous and then take it back for transmission from the chalet at Caux. This was time-wasting, and there was always danger that her frequent journeys might arouse suspicion in the minds of the Swiss police, who had probably not forgotten the Alex incident. Sonia's set was therefore moved to a chalet near Geneva until a better and more permanent home could be found for it.

At about the same time (August 1940) Moscow ordered me to move to Geneva and there train a wireless operator for Rado so that he could be independent of Sonia's set. This was the first time I met Rado. During the whole of my stay in Switzerland I never saw the inside of his house and he never entered my flat. We always met at agreed rendezvous at some "neutral" spot (i.e., a place where we were both comparatively unknown). Switzerland is not a large place, and after a time it became increasingly difficult to discover a new town to go to, which was not extremely inconvenient for one of us. Such are the minor burdens of a spy's life.

Rado had selected his recruit for training as an operator, and shortly after my arrival in Geneva I was put in touch with "Edward." Edward, or, to give him his real name, Edmond Hamel, was a member of the Nicole Party of Geneva. This party, headed by Leon Nicole, was plainly left-wing and contained a large number of "fellow travellers" but was not officially a Communist party. It did, however, provide a fruitful recruiting ground for Rado, and Leon Nicole himself acted as one of Rado's chief recruiting agents. It was through him that Hamel was brought into the fold.

Hamel had an excellent cover for his activities as an operator, for he ran and owned a wireless shop at 26 Rue Carouge in Geneva. He was also a radio mechanic and wireless enthusiast, so he had a flying start for his new career—or rather side line. His wife Olga (cover name "Maude") was also a member of the Nicole Party and was recruited at the same time. They both knew that they were working for the Russians but did not really believe it at first, basing their disbelief on the fact that the operator to whom they were sending was so inefficient that they could not believe he was in Moscow!

The Hamels' flat made an admirable hiding place for Sonia's set, and we moved it from the chalet and installed it above the shop. Sonia and I worked it for the first few months ourselves, she coming over from Caux for the purpose while I trained Hamel so that eventually he could take over.

Sonia had become increasingly restless and had repeatedly asked Moscow for permission to leave Switzerland and return to England. It was not until November, when Moscow could see that the hand-over had worked satisfactorily and that Sonia's group was now firmly in liaison with Rado's and communication with Moscow assured, that she received permission to leave. On December 20 Sonia left for London on her British papers. I do not think that since that time she has had any connection with a Russian spy net. She had been too disillusioned by the Russo-German pact to want to go on working and was only too thankful to sink back into respectable obscurity. Moscow on their side were obviously worried both by the Alex incident and the denunciation by Lisa Brockel and were, I think, equally thankful to let her go. They knew that as a loyal Party member she would not talk. There are no Kremlin objections to retirement from the service if circumstances permit and discretion is maintained. Vengeance is reserved for those who talk or who fall by the wayside for people like Rado and me. Inefficiency and loquacity are the capital crimes.

Before Sonia left she had received from Moscow a new code and new schedules and call signs which she handed over to me. At the same time she told me that I had been ordered to move back to Lausanne and set up a transmitter there to carry part of Rado's traffic as soon as Hamel had built a new transmitter and was a proficient operator. The building of a set was an easy matter for the efficient radio mechanic, and by the beginning of December his set was ready and tested. As an operator, Hamel still left much to be desired, and I left Bill Philips in his flat to assist him until he could carry on by himself. Bill had only one desire—to return to England and rejoin Sonia—but this I could not allow until the organisation could carry on without him. So he remained with Hamel until March, by which time the latter was trained sufficiently. Bill then pulled out of the organisation, and though he remained in Switzerland until 1942 he had no more official contact with us after March 1941. Moscow allowed him to try to make arrangements to leave at the end of 1941 and even assisted him in obtaining a British passport by getting a leading British politician to intervene on his behalf. The politician concerned acted, I am sure, quite innocently in this as Moscow worked through a number of cut-outs, and the person in question would probably have been horrified at the thought of assisting a Russian spy.

On December 15, 1940, I left Geneva for Lausanne, which was to remain my headquarters until I found a less comfortable abode in a Swiss prison cell.

It was not easy to find an apartment in Switzerland in those days, for with the fall of France and the Low Countries there had been an influx of refugees, many of them with money to burn, and there was an acute housing shortage. It would have been obviously impossible to install myself in a hotel or pension. Things were not made easier by a police decree which forbade foreigners to rent apartments and insisted that they should live in hotels. The motives for this ordinance were partially for security but principally mercenary. The war had killed the tourist-trade and the Swiss were reluctant to see their hotels standing empty when they could be filled with rich refugees who would probably spend more money in a hotel than they would in an apartment.

I decided to ignore this order and take a flat first and argue about it afterwards. After some difficulty I managed to find a suitable one in a big block at 2 Chemin de Longeraie. It was self-contained and sufficiently commodious, so I was independent of the rest of the world. It also had the advantage of being alone at the end of a short corridor so that I could hear the footsteps of anyone approaching, thus allowing a minute's grace before the doorbell rang.

Having installed myself, the next thing was to install the transmitter, which I had brought over from Geneva, wrapped up in my dirty laundry. It was in the highest degree unlikely that anyone would stop and search me or my baggage, but the extra precaution cost little. The flat was admirably suited, in another way, for my less legal purposes, as it was but one floor from the top, and the roof of the block overtopped all the neighbouring buildings. Ideal as the setup was, it still took me almost three months to establish contact with Moscow.

Most accounts of spies and secret activities skate lightly over the purely physical routine difficulties of the trade. Such accounts are generally concerned with the details of the hero's cunning in outwitting the activities of the police. In real life, once the police are really after you, there is little you can do to avoid them. The average spy hopes to avoid police notice rather than to evade it once it is awakened. His real difficulties are concerned with the practice of his trade. The setting up of his transmitter, the obtaining of his funds, and the arrangement of his rendezvous. The irritating administrative details occupy a disproportionate portion of his waking life and cut unwarrantably into his hours of sleep.

I had my flat and I had my transmitter, and the rest should have been easy. Unfortunately, here I came up against Swiss rules and regulations. There was a ban on the erection of any kind of external aerial on a building. Sonia had not encountered this problem, as a wire strung over the roof of her chalet at Caux out in the country would have excited no notice and, if it had, little comment. Not so in the heart of Lausanne. Again I decided to take the legal bull by the horns or rather in this case ignore his existence altogether. Adopting the air of an idiot and foreign child, I went to a wireless shop near by and explained that I wished them to erect an aerial for my wireless set in my fine new flat. I explained, unnecessarily, as my French accent was not impeccable by any means, that I was English and, exiled as I was from my own country for the period of the war, I was naturally anxious to keep in the closest touch with events at home and therefore wanted to listen to as many English broadcasts as possible. I explained that as my French was bad the short-wave continental broadcasts were not satisfactory and anyway they were designed for foreign consumption. I wished to listen to the medium-wave broadcasts put out by the B.B.C. for the English themselves, and these I could not get on my set with an indoor aerial. I do not know to this day whether my set with the aerial I eventually got would have enabled me to hear the ordinary B.B.C. home programme—nor, indeed, whether I could not have heard it anyway with an ordinary indoor aerial strung round my room. Luckily the mechanic in the shop was equally ignorant—or supremely indifferent—and after the usual delays which afflict workmen all over the world when labour is in short supply, he consented to come round and try to fix something up.

On his arrival a new and unexpected difficulty presented itself. The honest little man had apparently fallen for my story in a big way and was determined, law or no law, that I was to have the best aerial Switzerland could provide to enable me to listen to the programmes of my choice and of my native country. He had brought with him a large and superior aerial with every known device and side wire designed to cut out all possible interference. This would have been delightful had I really wanted to listen to the home news from London but quite disastrous for transmitting home news to Moscow. All I needed was a straight aerial of the right length with no devices to frustrate *les parasites* (as the French so delightfully call interference). In fact, in my own small way I desired to increase the number of parasites on the air by my own efforts. Ultimately, after endless explanation and liberal administrations of whiskey (of which luckily I had a large stock), I managed to get him to erect a straight aerial to suit my purpose. I do not think that he suspected anything. He went away quite certain that the

English were, as he had always been told, quite mad; but he had enough scotch inside him to allay his suspicions.

I took the precaution, for a week or so, of hiding the parts of my transmitter carefully in the flat: one piece in the mattress of my bed and another behind the bath, just in case I had been denounced and was raided. Nothing so drastic happened, though I did receive a visitor who arrived most opportunely during this period, when my flat had an appearance of absolute innocence and my actions were those of the character I was pretending to be—an Englishman, stranded in Switzerland by the war, with ample leisure and ample funds. Lausanne was full of such, ranging from the genuine, stranded resident or refugee down to the frank *embusqué* who had no intention of returning to England and military service and every intention of passing a comfortable and neutral war. I attempted to steer a graceful course between both extremes, my air of respectability being counteracted by my being obviously of military age.

The bell rang one evening and I opened the door to a polite, solid gentleman in the plainest of plain clothes who in no country in the world could have been anything other than what he was—a policeman in mufti. On such occasions as this the best course is to leave all the running to the other person—especially as I was conscious that only the minutest search of the place would show anything suspicious and that my papers, which I showed him, were in perfect order. He took the proffered seat and cigar and explained, in the politest way, that there was an ordinance that forbade foreigners to rent apartments, and perhaps I would be good enough to explain myself. I decided that a mild bluff and an appeal to Swiss cupidity was the only possible course. I explained that I had not been aware of the order when I took the apartment and had only learnt of it too late. I added that I understood that the main reason was to ensure that the hotels remained full and that there was no diminution of the revenue to the Swiss national exchequer from foreigners. I was perfectly prepared to give up the flat, inconvenient as it would be, and retire to a hotel, but felt that I must point out that it was an expensive flat in an expensive block of flats and that I was spending far more occupying it than I would living qui-etly *en pension* in a hotel. I was a man of some means and simple pleasures and I was sorry that the means of gratifying them, namely by living alone in a flat rather than crowded into a hotel, were to be denied me, especially as any change in my present mode of life would decrease the flow of sterling from my pocket into the Swiss coffers.

I hardly hoped that the line would work, but I put it over with all the conviction I could and reinforced it with another dose of my invaluable whiskey. Swiss thrift overcame police prudence. He asked me if I would be prepared to divulge my financial position. With a show of some reluctance at having to produce such private matters I explained that I was in receipt of sixty-five pounds a month from England and in addition had a balance of some fifteen thousand Swiss francs in the bank. I added that I was of course prepared to have this investigated if he so desired, but naturally I would prefer to avoid the possible embarrassment of police enqui-ries of my bank manager. He was kind enough to accept my word and pressed for no more factual details. This was, on the whole, as well since my total finances at that moment amounted to five hun-dred dollars which I had in my pocketbook. The network was then in low financial water and the monthly remittance and the sub-stantial balance were figments of my fancy.

Pressing my advantage, I asked if I could have permission to remain in the flat for the next six months. This I got; and it was renewed afterwards every six months without question. I wrote a standard letter stating that I was still in receipt of this entirely notional sixty-five pounds a month, and by return post came the permission. This was one of the few occasions when I had to bluff and trust to luck. It worked, and I had overcome the two main hurdles a spy has to surmount. I had a fixed and legal base, and my means of communication were secured. These two obstacles trip up ninety per cent of the spies who end their lives on the scaf-fold or in the cells. The victims are caught either through their means of communication—by radio monitoring or censorship—or because they have been unable to legalise themselves in the country where they are operating. It is practically impossible to be an efficient spy and be, at the same time, perpetually on the run. It was not too bad for me, as the worst that I had to expect from the Swiss was a period of imprisonment; while, if I failed to get established, I could always go quietly to ground with one of Rado's friends who had little to fear—the penalty for sheltering a spy in a neutral country being comparatively slight. Admittedly I was caught in the end, and caught through my means of communication like most of the rest. But thanks to the thrift of the Swiss and the mellowing effect of scotch whiskey I had almost three years' run for my money.

With myself legalised and the aerial installed I had merely to get the set working and contact Moscow. This was not too easy. I had already spent six weeks in dealing with the police and getting my dilatory mechanic on to the job and now I was anxious to get the set going without delay. But when I resurrected the bits of the transmitter from their hiding places and set the whole thing up, the crystal refused to oscillate. After a great deal of trial and error (after all I was not a trained radio mechanic and Hamel and his professional advice were not available to me in Lausanne) I managed to get the set to work by shortening the lead-in and installing the apparatus in the kitchen. This was not in the least convenient, but it was safer, as it ensured me against casual interruption, for it was unlikely that any unwanted guest who arrived during my transmitting times would penetrate to the kitchen. At least I could do my best to stop him and the arrangement saved my having to think up an easy and quick way of hiding the transmitter, which would have been necessary had I installed it, as I had at first wished, in my living room.

With the set now working, I had only to contact Moscow, and in my innocence I imagined this would be an easy task. Night after night, with my receiver tuned to the wave length given me in my schedule, I called at the arranged times. My tappings went out onto the unreceptive ether. Moscow could not or would not hear. Several times I almost decided to give up for the moment and go to

Geneva and ask Rado to put a message over his set—which I knew now to be working in Hamel's flat—asking Moscow to listen carefully and let Rado know if I was getting through or whether the set was still faulty. I banished this temptation, as the one thing we were anxious to do was to keep the two sets as unconnected as possible. I settled down again with renewed patience and continued calling. It was all the more irritating because the whole time I could hear Moscow calling me: "NDA NDA NDA," but they continued merely to call and I could get no indication that they could hear me, merely the perpetual reiteration of the call sign, as maddening to taut nerves as a dripping tap.

Persistence, however, won its ultimate reward. On March 12 for the thousandth time I tapped out the call sign "FRX FRX FRX." Then through the hum and crackle of static and over the background noise of other signals I heard "NDA NDA OK QRK 5." (QRK 5 indicated in the "Q code" that my signals were being heard very strongly.) Contact had been established.

7

BLUEPRINT FOR ESPIONAGE

There now follows a description of the layout of a Red Army espionage network in theory. It is the blueprint which all networks abroad attempt to follow. I can of course speak only for the Red Army system, as that is the only one I know. I should imagine that the Red Fleet or N.K.V.D. (now M.V.D.) network would be organised on approximately the same lines. It is, in fact, an eminently practicable, simple, and effective system, giving the maximum degree of efficiency with the minimum danger of compromise.

The head of the network is, of course, the resident director. Except in exceptional circumstances, he does not reside in the country against which his network is operating but lives and directs the organisation from a convenient neighbouring country against whose interests he is forbidden to work. It naturally happens on occasions that a resident director obtains information concerning his country of residence. In such cases, in normal times, he would hand the development of the source over to another resident director whose network was directed against the first director's country of residence. For example if the resident director in Switzerland of the network against Germany discovered a source who was capable of producing information from the Swiss General Staff, he would hand the source over to the resident director of the network working against Switzerland, who would probably be resident in France, and leave the latter to work out ways and means of getting the information to Moscow. The reason for this is obvious. The local police or counterespionage authorities are likely to take a much greater interest in the activities of anyone they suspect of working against them than they are in an individual who, while resident in their country, is working against a foreign power. Also the chances of compromise through treachery or double agents are much greater if the resident director is living, as it were, on top of his sources. It is, in fact, an extension of the old maxim about dirtying one's own doorstep.

The resident director is also, usually, not a native of his country of residence. He is usually not a Russian either, and in fact few Soviet nationals are used in Russian espionage networks. The Centre (i.e., Moscow) finds that the difference between the way of life in Russia and other countries is so great that it is difficult for Soviet citizens to adjust themselves. Also a Soviet citizen is a much more likely target for suspicion than a person of another nationality. It used to be said that "every Japanese is a spy." This applies equally well to Russians, as it is impossible for a Russian to get abroad until he has been checked and double-checked by the N.K.V.D. and is known to be one hundred per cent politically reliable. This is equally well known to all foreign counterespionage authorities, who as normal routine take a considerable interest in the activities of any Russian national in their midst.

The resident director is also usually forbidden to search for and develop sources of information. It is not for him to recruit agents or to conduct operations. His tasks are to control the communications system, cope with finance, sort out, evaluate, and edit the information that comes in to him, encipher it for onward transmission to the Centre, and generally to supervise and conduct the work of the whole organisation; seeing that the right lines are being developed and exploited at the right time, but keeping in the background and restricting knowledge of his identity to the minimum number of people. He is usually unknown to his agents, couriers, and radiotelegraphists, maintaining contact with them only through his liaison agents or "cut-outs," who are the only people aware of his identity.

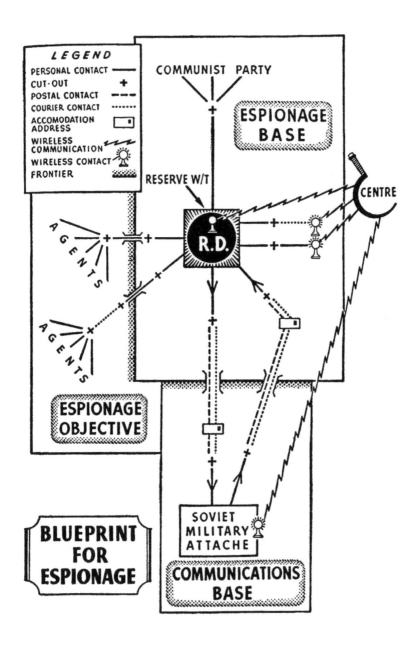

Under the resident director come the cut-outs, who bear the heat and burden of the day. They may or may not be natives of the country of residence of the director or of the country against which the network is working, depending on circumstances and their own particular ability. They act as "talent spotters" and if necessary recruiters as well. It is usually preferable for the actual approach to a new source to be made by another cut-out, one removed from the principal liaison agent, as this reduces the risk of compromise.

One of the most important sources of information and one of the main recruiting grounds for agents is of course the local Communist Party, referred to in network jargon as "the Neighbour." (Not to be confused with "the Neighbours," in the plural, which means the Comintern or rather the function which continued in Russia after the Comintern had been officially, and of course only in theory, abolished.) In every Communist Party there is one highly placed official whose main task is to gather information gleaned from Party members and fellow travellers and pass it on to the resident director through the main cut-out, who is in close but secret touch with him. It is this official who keeps an eye open for likely and useful recruits and passes their names on to the cut-out. The majority of agents are recruited through this means, and in any case any name forwarded by the network to Moscow for vetting is always referred back to the local Party for their views.

Another useful function of the Neighbour is the organisation of study and discussion groups among young students and intellectuals. From among the members of these groups it is possible to discover likely potential spy material: people who, though not members of the Party, are likely to be amenable to an espionage approach, and people who are either in, or likely one day to be in, posts where they could obtain information of value to Russia. Such promising candidates would be discouraged from openly joining the Party or openly expressing Communist or left-wing views. This ensures that their backgrounds are innocuous should they ever come under suspicion or be checked up by the counterespionage authorities. Such characters are sometimes paid for information which is valueless to the Centre purely in order to keep them on a string in the hope that one day they may advance in their profession and be in a position to supply really vital information. The network is prepared to wait a long time for its information to mature. It is much better, if the time can be afforded, to let your spy work his way gradually up into a position of trust rather than to be forced to make a pass at someone in a high position with the risk of failure or compromise. "Catch 'em young" is a motto which applies as well to espionage as to other walks of life.

Once an agent is recruited from the Neighbour, he passes his information direct to the cut-out and severs all connection with the Party intelligence system. His final recruitment will usually take place only after a long period during which time he will not be in touch with the network at all but will be passing his information through the contact in the Party. His material and his background will be checked and double-checked against other information supplied from similar sources and the Party records. Only then will he meet the cut-out and become part of the network. Even then he will be able to compromise only his own particular contact who, if he is arrested, will also be knocked off—but will not compromise the network as a whole.

Apart from agents, which term I have used in this chapter only to cover individuals who actually supply information—spies in the strictest sense of the word—the Party also is a recruiting ground for radiotelegraphists and minor cut-outs and couriers. These may be of the nationality of the country against whom the network is operating or in which the resident director is living. The sole task of the couriers and minor contacts is to act as channels for the information from the agent himself to the resident director, and vice versa. In most cases (and this is of course desirable as often as it is feasible) they are unaware of the identity of the agent they contact or the cut-out to which they work, merely meeting them at predetermined times and places and never at their homes. The information or instructions that they carry are either memorised or typewritten. In the latter case the message is typewritten through a well-used bit of carbon paper and the carbon copy is carried and the original is destroyed. This method makes it much harder to identify the typewriter upon which the message was written should it fall into unauthorised hands. The carbon copy is of course destroyed as soon as the resident director has incorporated it into his enciphered message.

As stated, liaison between the resident director and the local Communist Party is usually carried on by the chief cut-out, who is naturally a person in whom both parties have complete confidence. However, on certain occasions when important directives are being transmitted from Moscow, a secret meeting is arranged between the resident director and the Party leaders where the matter can be discussed. This is one of the few occasions when a director comes out into the open, and happens very rarely.

In all agents' messages and in all enciphered texts, only cover names are used for the sources, etc., and the messages are couched in a jargon which would make them difficult of interpretation by anyone not "in the net," so even if the gist of the message could be made out the agent's identity is concealed by the use of the cover name. The resident director has to memorise all the cover names used in his network. English Christian names are most commonly used, and both male and female names are employed indiscriminately without regard to sex: thus a male agent may easily have a female cover name. In cases where a source is only casual and not in frequent use, the director may give him a name which can be easily remembered by association—such as "Red" if he has red hair or "Lanky" if he is very tall. This is used only for unimportant characters whom the director might not easily be able to remember, and is a practice which is discouraged by Moscow, as such a cover name is obviously less secure than a purely arbitrary one.

In addition to persons, countries also have cover names as well and these vary from network to network. In the Swiss network against Germany, Great Britain was "Brazil," France "Florence," Germany "Jersey," and so on. The U.S.S.R. was always "Home." Other institutions and objects also had their own names. In my network a wireless transmitter was a "musical box"; a passport a "shoe"; a forger of false passports thus naturally became a "cobbler"; a prison was a "hospital" and thus the police became the "doctor."

Finance is one of the major responsibilities of a resident director. He is responsible for paying the entire network and submits his accounts to the Centre once a year. He also has to send an estimated budget for the next year's expenditure. This yearly grant is seldom paid in a lump sum, but at least twice a year the director sends a courier to a neighbouring country where he meets a courier from the Centre who hands the money over, always in dollars. This the director is forbidden to put in a bank; he keeps the entire sum in dollars, hidden somewhere, and removes what is necessary from time to time to change it into local currency for immediate expenses. He is, however, sometimes allowed to put the money in a safe-deposit box.

Salaries in a Soviet espionage network bear little if any relation to the work performed. Instead they are based on the amount the individual needs to maintain his position and support his dependents. Thus the anomaly frequently occurs of an old and trusted agent who is doing valuable and dangerous work being paid far less than, say, a cut-out who has been newly recruited but who has a certain position in life to maintain if he is not to come under suspicion.

A resident director receives about two hundred and fifty to five hundred dollars a month, depending on his dependents, his social position, and the cost of living in the country concerned. A wireless operator under the same conditions would receive from a hundred to two hundred dollars a month. If, on the other hand, he or she has a regular job as well, all that would be paid would be the actual expenses of the job. Agents are paid by results, but an agent of long standing who has produced consistently good and voluminous information may also receive a fixed retainer. Bonuses are also paid for exceptionally good pieces of work. The rates of pay are based on the amount of money that the member of the network has to expend from his day-to-day living expenses. The Centre does not encourage overpayment, as this might result in the individual's accumulating a large bank balance. This is regarded as undesirable, for not only is it a waste of Soviet government money but it also increases the risk of the person's "going private" (i.e., leaving the organisation).

Full-time members of a spy ring are told that they are fully and regularly embodied members of the Red Army and as such can receive military decorations for meritorious service. What actually happens is that all the agent gets is the promise of such a decoration if and when his work outside Russia is finished. For example Rado was a full colonel in the Red Army and I was a major, and when I was in Moscow I was told that I would be promoted to lieutenant colonel on my next assignment. At various times I was informed that I had been recommended for three Soviet decorations, the only one specified being the Order of the Red Banner. This I got for inventing a simplified system of sending Morse numbers which cut transmitting time by a third. I am still, not unnaturally, awaiting my investiture!

In theory a member of the network can retire on full pay after five years' service abroad—but his pension will be paid only in roubles in Russia. And in practice, if he did try to live in idleness and ease on his pension in Russia, he would soon get into trouble, as the slogan "He who does not work shall not eat" would be enforced—even for spies on full pay. He would find it more convenient—and certainly healthier—to volunteer for a further tour of duty abroad or hastily to find some other employment within Russia.

In addition to the return to Russia at the end of the five-year tour, agents are also sometimes summoned back to Moscow either for discussions or to take a course in some specialised subject. In such cases the individual travels to some other country—usually one with a common frontier with the U.S.S.R.—and there, at a prearranged rendezvous, he meets an agent from the Centre who hands him a new passport (sometimes a Russian one) containing the necessary visas—and of course in a false name. In return, the recalled spy hands over to the Centre's agent a sealed envelope containing his original passport and necessary documentation which he receives back on his return from Russia.

Frequently these sudden recalls to Moscow are not dictated by necessity but from a desire by the Centre to ascertain the reactions of the person to such a summons. If he expresses immediate willingness to return, the instructions are, as often as not, cancelled at the last minute. If, however, he hesitates or suggests that his recall might imperil the working or security of the network, Moscow's suspicions are at once aroused. He then becomes suspected by the Centre of "Trotskyist sympathies" or some lesser crime, and in all probability is enticed to some other country whence he can be easily abducted to Soviet Russia or where he can be conveniently liquidated.

If the spy is of little importance and his knowledge of the network is limited, the Centre may not take such drastic action. If they decide that his "going private" will not imperil the organisation or hamper its main working, he may merely be excluded from the network, and those individuals with whom he has been in contact are withdrawn and posted elsewhere.

The only occasion on which a member of the network is given leave to get out of the country is if he is under suspicion by the authorities or his security is imperilled by some other member of the organisation who is under suspicion for double-dealing. In such cases, if the need is really urgent, he can even leave without the permission of the Centre. In these cases he will go to his "place of conspiracy" where he will be recognised by the other contact who is there for just such an eventuality. The contact will not, however, make contact on sight. He will note the person's appearance and report back to the Centre, which will then check up to see that it is the right man and not an impersonator planted by some counter-espionage authority. The Centre will also check up through the local party and the other members of the network as to the circumstances of the person's departure, and if they are satisfied, then, and only then, will contact be made at the "place of conspiracy."

A resident director, or any member of a network who holds a cipher known only to himself and the Centre, has another course open to him apart from going to the "place of conspiracy," in the event of his being forced to fly the country without receiving specific instructions from the Centre as to his future. He can go to any Soviet military attaché in any country other than that in which he is resident—the farther away the better—and there, without revealing his identity, he hands in a message in his own cipher for the M.A. to dispatch. This message the M.A. will forward to Moscow, asking no questions but merely arranging a rendezvous some time ahead. Moscow will send in return a photograph of the agent and his "control questions." This is a form of question and answer known only to the Centre and the resident director concerned. The M.A. will go to the rendezvous and if the person tallies with the photograph and can give satisfactory answers to the control questions, then his *bona fides* is considered to be satisfactorily established and the fugitive resident director will receive further instructions.

So far I have described the skeleton of the organisation and the functions of its main component parts. Also the way its members are recruited, its relations with the local Communist parties, and the means by which information flows to the resident director have been outlined. No mention has been made of the most vital and probably the most difficult operation of all—the getting of the information to Moscow. Communications are the most important part of any spy ring and are its Achilles heel, as it is by tapping in on these that the counterespionage authorities gain most of their information and obtain most of their successes. Because of its importance I have left this subject to the last. Without communications with the outside world and thus to its headquarters, the most efficient spy ring in the world is powerless—as Rado found to his cost in 1940. Cut the channels of communication and you have rendered the network useless. In all probability its attempts to open up communications on an extemporised basis will betray its workings, and the individuals can be scooped up at leisure. This is, I have no doubt, the axiom of counterespionage authorities throughout the world.

Every resident director has of course his own separate means of communication. Before the war the normal means of transmitting the information which the resident director had received, sifted, and evaluated was by means of microphotographs. The director enciphered his text and then the messages were divided into portions of about five hundred cipher groups each. These portions were then microphotographed and resulted in a negative about the size of a pinhead. The pinhead negative was then stuck on an ordinary postcard, the position on the postcard being naturally agreed beforehand. The postcard, which bore a perfectly innocent and normal message, was then sent by the resident director to an address in a nearby country where it was collected by a courier and delivered, either direct or through yet another cut-out, to the Soviet military attaché, who sent it on either in the diplomatic bag or over embassy wireless channels.

Similarly, if the Centre wished to communicate with a resident director, a postcard carrying microphotographs would be sent in the bag to the military attaché's office in a country adjacent to that in which the resident director concerned lived. This postcard the military attaché sent to an accommodation address in the resident director's country where it was collected by a courier and delivered to the chief cut-out, who in turn delivered it to the resident director. In all cases the occupiers of the accommodation or "cover addresses" concerned were entirely ignorant of the identity of the resident director, the military attaché, or even of the cut-outs who collected the mail. They usually believed that they were merely acting as accommodation addresses for the local Communist Party by whom they had probably been recruited.

Apart from this system of microphotographic communication, the networks also used a courier system. The resident director would send one of his trusted cut-outs to various fixed rendezvous in neighbouring countries where the cut-out would meet a courier from the Centre. This system, if slightly slower, was obviously better for the transmission of bulky documents or samples of apparatus

These two systems worked very well in times of peace, when postal communications were easy and rapid and, generally speaking, there was no systematic censorship of mail. In time of war, when communications were disrupted, at best subjected to long delay, and at worst never arrived at all, the system was clearly impracticable, and, save over short distances, broke down. Even when it worked, all correspondence was liable to severe scrutiny by wartime censorship with the consequent risk of compromise.

As a result there was a radical reorganisation of communications systems, and now the main system in use is short-wave wireless transmission. This system is obviously infinitely quicker than the accommodation address and the numerous cut-outs and, provided normal precautions are observed, is equally safe.

In wartime it was vital that the Centre receive information as quickly as possible. Most of the information transmitted by networks concerned operational matters, and these would have been useless even if they had been subject only to the normal peacetime postal delays. As a result wireless transmission was instituted as the normal means of communication between the resident director and the Centre; and all resident directors are now required to undergo a course in radiotelegraphy and construction in Moscow before taking up the direction of a network abroad. Directors so qualified can send off urgent information as soon as it is encoded, without having to contact the normal wireless operator. If the director is forced to flee the country he can then build a new transmitter and is thus in a position to contact the Centre without the delays which a "place of conspiracy" or the contacting of a military attaché is bound to entail.

Though resident directors are now required to be so technically efficient, this newly acquired art has not taken away from the importance of the networks' wireless operators. Even if the director can transmit, it is obviously highly undesirable that in normal circumstances he should go to the set and do it himself—or worse still have the set in his house and transmit from there himself and thus imperil the whole network. As a result there is need for reliable wireless operators who will probably know the chief cut-out but will not know the identity of the director himself.

The ideal operator, like a resident director, is not a native of the country in which he is working. Through being a foreigner it is easier for him to hide his nocturnal and clandestine activities than if he were a permanent resident with many friends and relations all idly curious as to how he spends his time. In equally ideal circumstances this ideal operator will install himself and his transmitter in a top-floor flat of a large building situated in a built-up area. This makes it harder for direction-finding apparatus to locate him than if he were in an isolated place.

In peacetime the operator would probably have no more than two days a month when he was bound to establish two-way contact with the Centre. In addition there would also be several days each week when the Centre would be listening, at prearranged fixed times, in case he should call. Also on certain fixed days the operator himself would be required to listen in in case the Centre wished to call him.

In my network the Centre used a fixed call sign, though the call signs used by our sets varied according to a prearranged schedule. In order to establish communication a fixed call wave was used. For example, if I wished to call the Centre I would tap out my call sign in Morse on my fixed call wave, say 43 metres. The Centre would be listening and reply on its fixed call wave, perhaps 39 metres. On hearing the Centre reply, I would then switch to my working wave length, say 49 metres, and then with a different call sign send over my material. The Centre would similarly switch wave lengths and call signs, and move over to their working wave length. This system, though it may sound complicated on paper, was simple to operate in practice and cut to the minimum the possibility of radio monitoring.

All messages, of course, were always in cipher and the cipher was one that could be read only by the Centre and the resident director. In the case of our net things were slightly different since, as well as Rado, the resident director, I also held my own cipher, and as I had my transmitter in my flat I was able to answer any questions from the Centre often in a matter of hours. Modern ingenuity has also reduced the risk of having a transmitter on the premises. In the old days transmitters were bulky pieces of apparatus which could not easily be hidden. Now they are made so that they do not occupy more space than the average portable typewriter and are capable of disguise in various forms. Any good modern receiving set is perfectly suitable for picking up messages from the control station. So much for communications.

The foregoing account is an attempt to describe how the network is designed to work under ideal conditions, if it follows strictly the lines laid down by Moscow. Obviously circumstances must alter cases and the network must be adapted to fit in with local conditions, but the general plan is constant and, as will be seen, corresponds very closely with the network in Switzerland. Any variations were due to the exigencies of war and occasionally to the human factor—such as the frailties of the resident director himself. A comparison of the two diagrams showing the organisation in theory and in practice shows the similarity.

It may be argued that the above description of the ideal Soviet network bears little or no resemblance to the espionage organisation uncovered in Canada. There the whole case centred round the Soviet Legation in Ottawa itself, and the legation was directly concerned with espionage against Canada. This goes entirely contrary to the canons of classical Soviet espionage. There is, I think, an easy explanation for this, one which accounts for this variation from the normal—and also, I believe, for the comparative ease with which the network was uncovered. If the network had been properly run even the defection of Gouzenko should not have exposed the whole network. But in fact the network was an *ad hoc* affair set up in rather a hurry.

The reasons for this are not far to seek. At the outbreak of war the main Soviet espionage effort was switched to Germany and her satellites, and the networks working against the British Empire and the United States were allowed to lie fallow. With the German attack on Russia it became even more imperative to mobilise all espionage resources for the current struggle. Also it was obviously politically undesirable for there to be any chance of a worsening of relations between the Allies as might result from the uncovering of a Russian espionage ring working against one of Russia's own allies. As a result the Soviet spy rings working against the Allies were closed down or allowed to lie dormant.

When it was apparent to Russia that victory was only a matter of time and that her Western Allies were so involved in the war that a separate peace was out of the question, the Centre began to think of reviving their networks in the democracies, so that they would be in full working order when peace came and Russia would once more be in a position to obtain information of value to her from her quondam allies but real and ultimate adversaries—Great Britain and the United States. In the meantime, however, the old networks had fallen apart and the old resident directors had been moved to other posts. There was no time to establish new resident directors and as a result the rather haphazard organisation as exposed in the Canadian case came into being. I myself have no doubt that even though this network was paying dividends to the Centre in the shape of good and high-grade information, new resident directors were being established and were building up their networks quietly in the background. The world was sufficiently startled at the amount of information that the Canadian network was able to obtain. I myself have no doubt that the permanent network will do as well—if not a great deal better—if it is not doing so already. Only the network in Canada and portions of it in the United States have been exposed. It is a fair assumption that a similar emergency network existed in England also. Meanwhile the new resident directors should be well established, perhaps in Mexico and France, working and building up their networks against the United States and Great Britain. Time alone will show how successful they are.

8

THE BLUEPRINT IN ACTION

Having outlined the theoretical layout of a Soviet spy ring, it is now time to give the actual details of the Russian espionage network working against Germany. To a certain extent I am outrunning my narrative, as I did not learn some of the facts and details until much later in my career—some of them not till I went to Moscow. But in order to draw a clear picture of the whole organisation I have here assembled all the details that I learned at all stages. It will be noticed, and a glance at the diagram of the network will show, how closely the actual spy ring corresponds with the blueprint. It must be remembered that I am dealing only with the main espionage organisation directed against Germany and based on Switzerland. Before the outbreak of war there had been several other organisations—of which Sonia's had been only one. These had lost touch with Moscow and been gradually and in part incorporated into the main Red Army network—as had Sonia's. I can speak only of these subsidiary networks in so far as they came into contact with mine. I have little doubt that they were inactive during the war as none of them, save Sonia's, had any means of communication after the fall of France. The unexpectedly swift advance of the German armies threw the whole Russian setup into confusion and caused the amalgamation of the minor networks into the main Red Army organisation.

For the sake of clarity and to keep as closely as possible to the outline given in the previous chapter I have divided the characters roughly under the heads under which they fall in the blueprint.

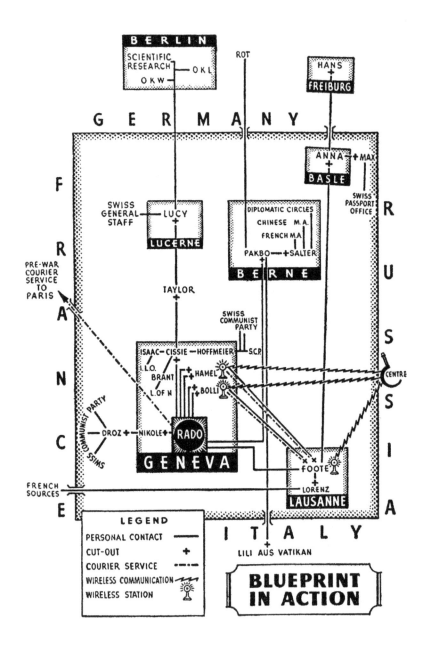

RESIDENT DIRECTOR

Alexander Rado. I have already described him and his ostensible cover occupation. He had, I think, come to Switzerland in 1937 and taken over the post of resident director from a woman known to me as "the woman major," whom I met afterwards in Moscow. He remained at the head of the organisation with me as his deputy until the arrests of the Hamels and Bolli in October 1943 forced him into hiding. After my arrest six weeks later the network was virtually quiescent until my release and journey to Paris a year later.

PRINCIPAL CUT-OUTS

Rachel Duebendorfer. Cover name "Cissie" or "Sisi." I did not meet her until after my release from prison, though Rado had been told by the Centre to put us into contact and we had a mutual place of conspiracy, where we were to meet if anything happened to Rado. She was, I should imagine, of Balkan origin herself though she held a Swiss passport, having gone through the ceremony of a *mariage blanc* with a Swiss in order to get Swiss papers. Her main function was to act as cut-out for Rado between her own two cut-outs, "Taylor" and "Isaac," mentioned below. She also acted as a contact between Rado and the Swiss Communist Party, as she was in touch with Hofmeier of that Party, who was, presumably, one of the Red Army contact men.

Cissie's role in the organisation was an important one and, as will be seen later, she also—at least in Moscow's view—played an important part in the Canadian spy case, as it was one of her more imprudent actions which, the Centre thought, led to the discovery of the Canadian network. Personally she was not really an attractive character, either physically or mentally. Her private life was slightly complicated as she lived with a former German politician, Boetcher, who had had to flee Germany after the Nazis came to power. He was living illegally in Switzerland and was ultimately arrested by the Swiss police for working for the Russians and the British. I cannot speak for the British side but he certainly was not connected with our network.

"Pakbo." The other main cut-out for Rado's organisation. I never knew Pakbo's real name, though we met frequently just before my arrest and after my release. He had been working for the Russians for many years and acted as one of the chief cut-outs and talent spotters of the organisation. His main specialty was contact with diplomatic circles in Berne, where he lived, and he also ran agents in diplomatic circles outside Switzerland. In the case of Pakbo, Rado did as he should, and put me in touch with him when he went into hiding.

Apart from the specific sources mentioned below, Pakbo was also in touch with several military attachés, including the Chinese, of whom he made use after the wireless link was broken by my arrest. On my departure from Switzerland for Paris Pakbo also asked me to deliver a message to the Soviet military attaché to the effect that one Lieutenant Colonel Thibault, the Vichy French military attaché in Berne, wished to be placed in direct touch with the Russians. Thibault stated that he had details of V-3 and wished to hand the plans over personally to the Soviet military attaché. I passed the message on but do not know what, if any, action was taken on it by the Centre.

The other main cut-out was of course myself, who also acted as one of the wireless operators for the group.

WIRELESS OPERATORS

The organisation had three wireless transmitters working after the German attack on Russia. One was run by me from Lausanne, another by the Hamels in Geneva; and the third, ultimately in Geneva, by one Margarete Bolli (cover name "Rosie").

At this stage I need say no more about myself and my activities as an operator. I have already given details regarding the recruitment and training of the Hamels. Rosie, like the Hamels, had been recruited by that invaluable and industrious talent spotter Nicole. I trained her in transmission in Lausanne in 1942 and she set up her transmitter at first in her parents' house in Basle. This led to certain domestic difficulties and after a time she and the set moved to Geneva.

MINOR CUT-OUTS

The only subsidiary contact of any importance was Taylor. He was not only a cut-out but an agent as well. He worked back to Rado through Cissie. He provided the network with a certain amount of gossip and information from the International Labour Office where he worked as a translator. By origin a German Jew, his real name was Schneider (of which his cover name was of course only an English translation). In himself he was of little importance to the network, but as the recruiter and contact of "Lucy," our link with the German high command (who was of such importance that I have thought it worth while to devote a chapter to his activities), he was of vital importance. He and only he knew Lucy's real identity, and it was therefore vital for the network to keep him working and happy. It is not everyone who acts as intermediary for an agent who has access to all the secrets of the Oberkommando der Wehrmacht, and Taylor was at first our only link. At a critical period of the war the Centre offered him a salary for life if he would give up his job with the I.L.O. and devote himself solely to being contact man for Lucy. The only stipulation that Moscow made was that Taylor should provide an address in the United States to which the money could be sent in a lump sum in dollars. This, unfortunately for him, Taylor was unable to supply. Despite this, however, he gave up his job with the I.L.O. and did nothing more save cut-out work between Cissie and Lucy. I think that he is still waiting for his money.

COURIERS

The only couriers of any importance of whom the organisation made use were Rosie, who as well as being an operator acted as courier between Rado and me and also between Rado and Pakbo and Maude, the wife of Hamel, who, herself a trained operator, also was a courier between Rado and me when the latter was too busy to make personal contact.

The above is the main internal communication network. Rado at the centre with his two main cut-outs, Cissie and Pakbo, with Taylor as a secondary contact to the former. Both Cissie and Rado had personal contact with Nicole, who in turn acted as contact with the left-wing Socialists and also one portion of the Geneva and Tessin Communist parties. Cissie was also the cut-out to Hofmeier of the Party. Communication with Moscow was assured through the three transmitters, and Rosie and Maude acted as couriers between Rado, Pakbo, and me.

Before Rado had access to Sonia's transmitter he was, of course, using the old microphotographic technique for the transmission of his information through a cover address in France, whence it was delivered to the Soviet Embassy in Paris. It was the fall of France which, as I have explained before, forced the Centre to put him and Sonia in contact so that communications could be maintained.

With the organisation for the communication and transmission of information clear, the actual sources of information can be examined. To give a catalogue of all the sources would be extremely tedious and, after this lapse of time, almost impossible for me. There were, if I remember correctly, some sixty sources, i.e., agents with cover names, who supplied information to the network. Many of these I knew only by their cover names and many of them, in their turn, merely provided occasional information. Here I give only the main sources from which Rado drew the material for his reports. They alone were more than sufficient to keep our three transmitters fully occupied. I was often so rushed that I had only time to read and encipher the messages, and no time at all to digest their content, and as a result was on the air for hours at a time, which of course offends all security canons and would lead to certain discovery in an enemy country. The "Bupo" (Bundespolizei, the wartime Swiss police security organisation) were either kinder or less efficient.

Cissie's main sources were three in number:

1. Isaac, by origin a Lithuanian Jew. He asserted that when Russia occupied the Baltic States he had applied to the Soviet Embassy in Paris for Soviet papers, having registered as a Soviet citizen. He also stated that he had been told to stay in Switzerland and not go to Moscow. He was of use to the organisation not only

as a source but also, being a member of the staff of the I.L.O. and therefore possessing quasi-diplomatic privilege, as a useful depository for compromising documents and as a "safe house." The information that he supplied via Cissie was mostly material from the League of Nations and the I.L.O. and generally dealt, not unnaturally, with political matters. He was never given a regular retainer but was paid only by results.

2. Another source of Cissie's was "Brant," who supplied a certain amount of material on League of Nations matters. He was, I believe, some sort of connection of Cissie's by marriage. He later left Switzerland for France, of which country he was a national, and, as far as I know, is now out of the whole racket.

3. Cissie's third and most important source was Lucy, through the medium of Taylor. She had, in addition, several minor sources and contacts who were of use to the network but these do not merit mention here and will appear only in the course of the narrative.

Pakbo also had three main sources and as well acted as occasional contact with Nicole and the Swiss Communist Party. Probably his main source was "Rot," an organisation in South Germany, which I suspect was closely tied up with the German Communist Party and had links into and with the Swiss Party. This source produced political, military, and economic information from South Germany. Occasionally the source also yielded information from Berlin.

I never knew much more about the organisation, but I should imagine that it was a small group in close touch with events in South Germany, occasionally receiving information from members of the group who were stationed in Berlin or elsewhere and came down to South Germany for leave. The information was never very "hot" and it probably reached Pakbo through a series of couriers. I also suspect that he did not organise these but that they were organised by the Party in Switzerland.

His other source outside Switzerland was one known to me only by the rather romantic name of "Lili aus Vatikan." This source, as the name suggests, produced diplomatic information from Italy in general and the Vatican City in particular. I never knew how it reached Pakbo but always assumed that it was via the diplomatic bag (the delay in receipt would fit that assumption), and that the source was some diplomat accredited to the Vatican City.

In Switzerland Pakbo had one main source of value. This was "Salter." His identity was never known to me but I suspect that he was a Yugoslav and from the type of information that he produced it might well have been the Yugoslav military attaché. Apart from providing information, Salter also acted as a rather tenuous link between Rado and the British. Salter was in touch with the British military attaché and it was through Pakbo and Salter that Rado put out his feelers for a possible "safe house" with the British should his position become untenable in Switzerland. Rado did this when he saw that the "heat was on" and that it was only a matter of time before he was picked up or had to go into hiding. He actually made his approach and received a favourable reaction from the British. Rashly, he also put the suggestion to the Centre—who turned it down at once and ever after suspected Rado of, at the best, leanings towards the democracies and at the worst downright treachery. An interesting example of the different attitude of "allies" allegedly fighting the same war against a common enemy.

My own sources also were three in number. This is mere coincidence and not any mystic belief by the Centre in the virtue of uneven numbers.

My first source was "May." She acted as cut-out between me and Humbert Droz of the Swiss Communist Party. Droz had formerly been Secretary of the Comintern and had, in fact, preceded Dimitrov in that post. He had been previously in touch with another Russian network in Switzerland but had not had contact since 1939. I contacted him in 1941, on instructions from Moscow, who wished him to form his own network and supply such information as he could obtain from just over the frontier. This was not really a difficult or dangerous task as workers streamed to and fro over the German border with comparative ease, and there was an ample supply of Party comrades as potential recruits. Droz agreed to do this, but before he could take any steps he was arrested by the Swiss authorities for secretly reforming the Swiss Communist Party. He was released a few months later but abandoned the Communist Party and joined the Social Democrats, of which party he later became Secretary.

Helena Schmidt was a most useful source and veteran of the network, which had employed her for some twenty years. She was the contact between the network and the "cobbler" (maker of illegal passports).

My third source was never really a source of mine but was rather an unpleasant incubus thrust upon me by the Centre. George and Joanna Wilmer (cover names "Lorenz" and "Laura") were old established members of the Russian Intelligence Service. Of allegedly Swiss nationality, they had been born in Russia and had worked abroad for the Centre since 1926, in France, Japan, and the United States. I was given their real name by the Centre, who instructed me to contact them and take and transmit their material. Unfortunately Moscow was unable to give me their address. By the intelligent use of the telephone directory (an invaluable source and one so frequently neglected by enquiry agents of all kinds) I managed to locate them in their villa near Lausanne. I was treated by them with the utmost suspicion at first, and it was only after a great deal of difficulty that I managed to get any material from them—and then it was of a very low-grade nature. They were both always trying to discover my real name and address, but I am glad to say without success. There is now no doubt that at some period prior to the war they had been "got at" by the German Intelligence Service and were working as "double agents" for the Germans, i.e., supplying false information to the Russians, which information had been supplied to them by the Germans. I warned Moscow repeatedly, and repeatedly expressed my doubts as to their *bona fides*, but the Centre would have nothing of it.

These then are the sources from which Rado obtained his information for the Red Army. Drawn from all walks of life and all nationalities, there is no common factor to account for their activities as spies for the Red Army. They were in the main efficient and loyal, and their efforts did in some way assist the Allied cause and lead to the defeat of Nazi Germany. Let them be honoured for that.

I now turn to the most valuable source that the network had—the one man who supplied information from the very heart of Germany, whose contacts extended not only into the Wilhelmstrasse and the Bendlerstrasse but also into all places of authority in the Third Reich—Lucy.

9
ONE AGAINST HITLER

Who was Lucy? He was the most important actor in this peculiar drama, but he never came into the limelight. His supporting cast can only be dimly seen and hazily described; their names unknown and even their roles are undefined. Lucy, snugly ensconced in neutral Switzerland, held in his hand the threads which led back to the three main commands in Germany and also could, and did, provide information from other German government offices. Where he got his information and how it came were his own secrets. Even his own identity was for a long time shrouded in mystery. I can only give the facts as known to me, and the deductions that I can draw. The rest of the story is Lucy's—and Lucy is not talking.

First of all—what did Lucy produce? The answer to this is simple. Lucy provided Moscow with an up-to-date and day-to-day order of battle of the German forces in the East. This information could come only from the Oberkommando der Wehrmacht itself. In no other offices in the whole of Germany was there available the information that Lucy provided daily. Not only did he provide the day-to-day dispositions on the eastern front, but also Lucy could, and did, provide answers to specific questions. It frequently happened that Moscow had lost sight of such-and-such an ersatz division. An enquiry was put through Lucy and in a matter of days the answer would be provided, giving the composition, strength, and location of the unit in question.

As far as Moscow was concerned, this was obviously the most important function Lucy could perform. Russia, fighting with its back to the wall and scraping up its last resources, was obviously vitally interested in trustworthy information regarding the armed forces ranged against her—and this Lucy supplied. Anyone who has fought a battle from the General Staff angle will know what it means to be able to place the flags of the enemy on the map and plan the disposition of one's own troops accordingly, in as complete confidence in the authenticity of the information as if one had been in the headquarters of one's opposite number. Lucy put Moscow in this position, and the effect of the information on the strategy of the Red Army and the ultimate defeat of the Wehrmacht is incalculable.

If Lucy had confined himself to producing information regarding the German Army, that would have been in itself sufficiently remarkable, and as such he could have amply justified himself in Soviet eyes. But his sources went further. Not only did he provide information on the troop dispositions, information which could only have come from the O.K.W. in the Bendlerstrasse, but he also produced equally good information emanating from the headquarters of the Luftwaffe and the Marine Amt, the German Admiralty. These last two sources were subsidiary, as the Centre was naturally primarily interested in troop movements; but Lucy could and did provide information on German aircraft and German naval shipping, and occasionally threw in reports on German economic and scientific production. For example, I remember that in 1941 he supplied information regarding the manufacture of flying bombs and plans for the construction of ten-ton rockets. In effect, as far as the Kremlin was concerned, the possession of Lucy as a source meant that they had the equivalent of well-placed agents in the three service intelligence staffs plus the Imperial General Staff plus the War Cabinet Offices.

However late such information was received from such a source, it was obviously of immense value. What increased the value was the speed with which the information reached us. One would normally think that a source producing information of this quality would take time to obtain it. No such delay occurred in the receipt of Lucy's information. On most occasions it was received within twenty-four hours of its being known at the appropriate headquarters in Berlin. In fact, barely enough time to encipher and decipher the messages concerned. There was no question of any courier or safe hand route. The information must have been received by Lucy over the air, and his sources, whoever they were, must have gone almost hotfoot from the service teleprinters to their wireless transmitters in order to send the information off. This speed was one of the factors that made the Centre distrust this source, and only after bitter experience did they accept it at its face value.

Who was the source and how did he come into the network? As always in espionage, the end is dealt with first. Lucy was introduced by Taylor, alias Schneider, sometime early in 1941. Taylor was apparently an old friend of Lucy's and introduced him to the Centre on one condition only—that he, Taylor, and only he should know the true identity of the source and that Moscow would not be told. The Centre was extremely suspicious and at first advised Rado to have nothing to do with it. Even after Lucy had disclosed the date of the German attack on Russia some two weeks in advance, and check-backs had shown that the information was correct, the Centre still refused to accept the information and insisted that it must be some kind of plant. Despite the Centre's attitude we continued to "plug" Lucy's information over to Moscow. Rado, in one of his few independent gestures of the war, was paying Lucy without prior sanction from Moscow and insisting that this information was valuable, and indeed vital, to the Russian cause. "Dripping water wears away the hardest stone," and in the end we managed to convince Moscow that this information was, to say the least, extremely valuable to them. Once they were convinced, they went for it in a really big way. Lucy was given seven thousand Swiss francs a month as a retaining fee plus special bonuses, and his information, at least all that which passed over my transmitter, had a suffix of one code group meaning "Urgent decipher at once." In fact in the end Moscow very largely fought the war on Lucy's messages—as indeed any high command would who had access to genuine information emanating in a steady flow from the high command of their enemies.

Moscow accepted Taylor's conditions and Lucy was to them a source of unknown origin—as indeed he was to all of us till some time after the dissolution of the network. As far as I know this was the only time Moscow ever accepted an unvetted source; in this case they were amply justified for their unorthodox action.

So much for how Lucy came into the net. As far as the Centre was concerned we forced the source upon them. To the best of my knowledge no one received any thanks for doing so.

Who was Lucy? The answer to that is simple—Selzinger. Who was Selzinger? The answer to that is not so easy. Before Hitler came to power Selzinger had been connected with the theatre in Germany, probably as a producer, and gained quite a reputation in his profession in Berlin. He was not a German himself, but a Czech. After the establishment of the Third Reich he fled to Switzerland. On arrival there he did his best to make his stay as permanent as possible and to this end used his sources in Germany to ingratiate himself with the Swiss. In a short time the Swiss General Staff realised his value and used him as their main source of information regarding the German Army's disposition against Switzerland. In return for his information, Selzinger was given permission to reside in Switzerland. Until the rape of Czechoslovakia Lucy worked for the Czech General Staff, so the secret of his sources may have lain in Prague.

The Swiss General Staff regarded him so highly that they not only used him as a source of information regarding German intentions towards Switzerland—which of course his incomparable sources could provide—but also used him as an "evaluator." That is, they asked him to evaluate the information they received from other sources on the German armed strength and acted on his decision. He ended up, in fact, as the assessor for the Swiss Director of Military Intelligence on all military information emanating from Germany.

Selzinger had apparently wanted to contact the network and had been introduced to Taylor by one of the latter's minor sources. He was certainly a source of Taylor's in 1941 and quite consciously provided the Centre with his information—even though the Centre did not believe it. He was of course simultaneously providing the Swiss General Staff with such information as he could obtain regarding German intentions against Switzerland and his dual role must be remembered in assessing his actions. Selzinger was a refugee in a neutral country and as such was obviously out to ingratiate himself with as many authorities as he could find—especially the authorities which gave him a safe lodgment. To this end he remained loyal to his Swiss masters—as loyal as he did to his Russian ones. Luckily for him, their interests never clashed.

I never met Selzinger until after my imprisonment when, through a cut-out, he expressed a desire to see me. He was, throughout my active career as a spy in Switzerland, merely a cover name whose sources were equally veiled in jargon. For example "Werther" was his name for the O.K.W. and "Olga" for the Oberkommando der Luftwaffe. Similarly, the Marine Amt and other government departments had their cover names.

Selzinger lived in Lucerne where he was known as a "publicist," the easy phrase that covers anything from a writer of pamphlets to a best seller.

What was the source of his information? Here I must enter into the field of pure speculation. I do not know; the Centre did not know; Taylor did not know; and the only person who did know was Selzinger himself, and he is not telling. Whoever his sources were, they were obviously high up in the Nazi hierarchy and the information reached Selzinger by wireless. Since the war there have been various books produced by various leaders of the so-called German "resistance" and in them there has been mention of a Communist cell within the German Air Ministry which was broken up sometime in 1942. It is possible that Selzinger's sources included this particular spy ring and that this was the only one that the Germans managed to discover, leaving his Wehrmacht and other sources inviolate. This is not a wholly satisfactory explanation as Selzinger's sources continued uninterruptedly long after this alleged spy ring in the Luftwaffe was eliminated. It would be logical to assume that there might have been a slight hiatus at the time of the Luftwaffe arrests in 1942—but no such hiatus occurred and the information continued to stream in.

A really suspicious-minded person might think that the whole thing was a gigantic double-cross by the Germans, who could have supplied Selzinger with a vast amount of authentic information in the hope that the occasional piece of false information would be accepted as well. There is one scrap of intelligence to support this thesis, and one scrap only. At the time of Timoshenko's Kharkov offensive in 1942 the Russians based this offensive almost entirely on the information that Lucy supplied. In this case the Russians found themselves in a trap and heavy losses ensued. If this had been one of many incidents resulting from Lucy's intelligence, the thesis that the whole thing was a German strategic double-cross would be more tenable. However, this was the only occasion that his information turned out not to be genuine. It is almost inconceivable that the Germans—if they had controlled the source of Lucy's original intelligence—would not have attempted to cash in on it to a greater extent. This did not happen and I think that this excludes the double-cross hypothesis. It is of course possible that Selzinger's intimate contact with the Swiss General Staff may have helped to supplement his information. Selzinger may not have been above peddling to the Russians such information as he obtained in his capacity as an "evaluator" of Swiss intelligence—his own sources in Germany having failed him.

The only clue that Selzinger ever gave as to his sources was when I saw him after my release from prison, when he stated that the purge which resulted from the attempt of July 1944 had considerably reduced the number of his sources. He did manage, however, to produce formidable documentation which he asked me to take with me to Paris for transmission to the Soviet Embassy there, and the purge and the resultant almost complete elimination of any potential resistance movement in Germany had obviously merely embarrassed and temporarily inconvenienced him rather than removed his sources. We can thus rule out any superpatriotic German general as the source.

Really, anyone's guess is as good as mine. If the source was a German double-cross it was a very badly conceived one. If it was the Bendlerstrasse they managed to continue very active even after sentence of death by the People's Court. If it was the Swiss they certainly showed more efficiency than they did in the elimination of our network.

Let the matter be left there. It is sufficient for my purpose—as it was for the Centre—that Lucy produced the "goods" and that on all occasions save one these were accurate, speedy, and complete. The war on the eastern front was fought largely on them and the intelligence produced led to victories for the Allies. I can only suggest that further enquiries be directed to Selzinger himself. As will be seen, he was arrested in June 1944 and released some three months afterwards with a certificate from the Swiss General Staff testifying to the services that he had performed and guaranteeing him immunity in the future. He is therefore presumably still a resident of Switzerland. His services in the past cannot be denied—he produced the answers and protected his sources, and one asks no more of a secret agent. His efforts, if any, in the future may be equally interesting. It is to be hoped that his skill at penetrating into the heart of general staffs remains confined to Germany—if his employers remain the same.

10

PRELUDE TO WAR

I have interrupted the story of my own activities in order to give a picture of a typical Soviet spy network and also to explain our own. Such background "briefing" is essential for the clear understanding of what follows. Without some background knowledge of the workings of a Russian spy organisation and the cardinal principles involved, many of my actions and the precautions that we took would appear meaningless and stupid. Anyone who has read so far will now appreciate the essential and elementary security precautions that were taken and the way that our sources were contacted. Later on it will be seen how criminal disregard for these "simple little rules and few" led the organisation into disaster.

The period of my career as an active spy when I was in direct wireless communication with the Centre in Moscow falls quite naturally into two parts. The first comprises the first few months of the spring of 1941, between the time that I at last established communication with Moscow on March 12 and the invasion of Russia by Germany on June 22. The second period is from the entry of Russia into the war until my arrest on November 20, 1943. The first period was really a continuation of the halcyon days of peace, after the outbreak of war in September 1939 when Philips, Sonia, and I had little to do and did it on the whole very well. The flurry caused by the fall of France had subsided, and Rado's communications were secure, thanks to the activities of Sonia and myself. He had one set working in Geneva operated by the Hamels and I was also in touch with the Centre from Lausanne. Life was pleasant and easy in Switzerland that spring, and I enjoyed it and the leisure to the full—it was the last leisure I was to have for some time.

In those easy, carefree days I had contact with Moscow twice a week only. Twice a week at one o'clock in the morning I would settle down at my transmitter and send off what little I had and receive Moscow's replies. I was not at that time asked to do any espionage work myself nor to go out and attempt to recruit sources. I was the substitute resident director and as such had to remain in the background; the Centre was perfectly content to know that I was there; that communications were secured and that if anything happened they could call upon me if necessary.

On instructions from the Centre I concentrated upon establishing myself so firmly in Lausanne that there would be no possible danger of my presence arousing suspicion. This was not easy, for in the middle of the war there were not a great number of British subjects of military age resident in neutral Switzerland. In normal times the Centre will often put a resident director into his country for two years before they ask him to take over any work: he spends the entire two years in building himself an impressive cover. I had to do this as quickly as possible, and in time of war. My fellow Englishmen varied from retired army officers and civil servants, who had settled down in Switzerland on their pensions and been caught by the war, to the riffraff of the Riviera, who had been swept out of France by the German invasion and had taken refuge in Switzerland where they lived precariously on their wits, the black market, and such remittances as they could get from home. The latter were not an attractive crowd but they turned out in the end to be useful to me—though quite unconscious that they were indirectly assisting the Red Army. I understand that I ended up with the reputation of being a mildly eccentric English millionaire who had managed to salt away a portion of his fortune abroad and who on the whole shunned the company of his fellow men. The reputation of wealth was essential as otherwise I might have had awkward questions from the Swiss police as to the source of my funds; indeed at times my finances were precarious, while at others I had tens of thousands of Swiss francs concealed in my flat. My reputation as a recluse was not ill deserved. If anyone has ever tried to encipher messages for half the night and transmit them for the other half he will understand the reason why for the rest of the day I was inclined to keep to my flat—and my bed.

At this time Rado's transmitter was capable of taking all the traffic that had to be sent, so I was not used as an overflow channel. Indeed, the only espionage assignment that the Centre gave me that spring was the task of preparing an economic report on Switzerland. This I agreed to do, but in fact did nothing about it as I had no qualifications nor indeed any sources at that time to produce such a thing. Moscow used occasionally to enquire solicitously as to its progress and I used to reply equally encouragingly but did nothing but look round in a vague sort of way for someone suitable to "ghost" such a report for me. Luckily, before Moscow became too querulous the German invasion took place and such academic matters were shelved.

Sonia had left, and Bill Philips, too, had left the net, so at that time my only espionage contact was Rado himself. Having finished training Hamel, I avoided him scrupulously to prevent compromise, though later Maude, his wife, was used as a contact in times of emergency or stress.

The main preoccupation of the network at that time was finance. An espionage organisation without finance is almost as useless as one without communications. The fall of France had cut Rado's purse strings and since that time he had been living on such monies as he could obtain from the Swiss Communist Party—who were now pressing for payment. The majority of my communications with Moscow at this time were over this financial question, and in the end it turned out that I had to do all the organisation for the financing of the network. Moscow were prepared to assist, but were quite unwilling or unable to suggest anything themselves save for one foolish suggestion and one abortive attempt.

Soon after establishing contact in March, after a long discussion with Rado I put the whole financial position to Moscow and asked for help and advice. The Centre replied by suggesting, help-fully, that I go to Vichy and collect money from the courier at a prearranged rendezvous; they added that if this was not possible I could no doubt arrange for a trusted go-between to go there in my place. I replied somewhat acidly that as things were in Europe at that time it was a little difficult for a British subject to go into Vichy France from Switzerland and in any case this would hardly be advisable as it would probably "blow" me completely or at least expose me and the network to a grave risk of compromise. As re-garded finding a reliable *homme de confiance* I had, as the Centre knew, no sources of my own at that time, having been told not to cultivate any, and by the time I had found someone reliable and had had him vetted by the Centre in all likelihood the whole net-work would, at best, be in the Swiss equivalent of Carey Street and, at the worst, in jail. The Centre tactfully dropped this suggestion and I heard no more about it; but in April or May they produced a further scheme.

I was informed that a courier was coming from Belgium and that he would meet Rado at a rendezvous in Switzerland and would hand over Rado's allocation of cash and also my own. The courier duly arrived—but empty-handed. He told the infuriated Rado that this was merely a trial trip to see what the frontier controls were like between Germany and Switzerland, and, having passed through them, he, the courier, was certain that this route was not practicable as the search was too stringent. To add insult to injury he attempted to borrow money from the almost penniless Rado in order to finance his return trip. After our experience of these two bright financial ideas by the Centre, it was obvious to Rado and me that unless we ourselves could think up some scheme for get-ting money and put it in words of one syllable to Moscow the whole organisation would crumble quietly into ruins.

I first of all suggested to the Centre that they should pay money into an account in my name in a foreign bank and that this sum could then be transferred in a normal way to me in Switzerland. This was at once turned down as it would be necessary for the cou-rier who paid the money to know my name, and this was strictly against the rules. They did state, however, that they could make cash payments into banks in Great Britain, the United States, China, and Sweden on receipt of instructions from me. They added, however, that on no account was the person receiving the money to know my name and the courier paying the money in would in turn give a false name. On those conditions and those conditions only could they help financially.

On the face of it, this did not look too promising. On the other hand the war had been going on some time and the various black bourses were in full blast. I made some discreet enquiries among my more monied Swiss friends and the shadier of my English acquaintances, and soon evolved a scheme which I thought would work. Through the agency of a Swiss friend I was able to get in touch with some firms which in the course of their normal business remitted money between Switzerland and the U.S.A. The usual procedure for such transactions was for the whole affair to be handled by the National Bank, which would change Swiss francs into dollars and vice versa at the rate of four francs thirty centimes per U.S. dollar. I proposed that, instead of doing their transactions through the normal and indeed only legal way, namely a Swiss bank, they should allow me to do them—at a cheaper rate.

The scheme was put up to Moscow and they agreed and played their part. The procedure was quite simple and almost foolproof. Moscow would pay into a bank in New York a sum of money in dollars for the credit of the Geneva account of an American firm. The firm's branch in Switzerland would be notified by telegram that this sum had been credited to their account and they would at once pay me the agreed rate in Swiss francs—at the black market rate.

This may sound complicated but in fact it was quite simple— and indeed profitable to all concerned. For ease and simplicity let it be assumed that the official rate for Swiss francs to dollars was four to the dollar and that the black market rate was two to the dollar (the real rates were 4.30 and at lowest 2.75 respectively) and that the sum in question was one hundred U.S. dollars. The Centre, through their courier, would pay into the firm's account at the New York bank the sum of one hundred dollars. The New York office of the firm would notify their Geneva branch that this sum had been credited to them in New York and that as a result they had a credit of four hundred Swiss francs or its equivalent available to them. The Geneva representative of the firm paid out to me two hundred francs (the equivalent of one hundred dollars at the black market rate). At the official rate of exchange, four Swiss francs to the dollar, he had thus paid out only fifty dollars and as a result he or his firm had fifty dollars' clear profit on the deal. The only loser was of course the Centre, which had to buy francs at a bad rate of exchange; but it enabled them (and it was the only way) to pay their network in Switzerland—and I suspect that the same system worked elsewhere. Thus everyone was happy. The firm in New York could not care less; their manager in Switzerland was making a handsome profit (the figures given above are of course arbitrary and put in for the sake of simplicity, but the mathematically inclined can work out the percentage of profit between rates of 4.30 and 2.75) and the Centre was able to finance its sorely embarrassed Swiss network.

This system was one which I worked satisfactorily all the time I was with the network, and as a result some hundreds of thousands of dollars were transferred to our use through the intermediary of innocent firms. The only limitation on the sums involved was laid down by Moscow. They stated that they were not prepared to do deals of more than ten thousand dollars at a time. Their reason for this was simple and practical. Any such transaction meant that a courier had to be given the money in question in cash to take to the bank and deposit. The Centre was not prepared to trust couriers with more than ten thousand dollars, as the temptation might prove too great and they might "go private" and settle down at large and at ease in a foreign democracy. Indeed one such case occurred and caused me considerable embarrassment.

My Swiss friend managed to get in touch with an American firm which was prepared to do business on these terms and he negotiated the first deal. The firm in question was an American one which had a flourishing business in Switzerland. I arranged over my transmitter that the Centre should send a courier from time to time to the bank in New York and pay ten thousand dollars into the firm's account for the credit of their Geneva branch. In due course Moscow informed me that the transfer had taken place, and also of course the firm's representative in Geneva was equally informed that this transfer to the credit of his account had taken place. When both sides were satisfied that the money was there, then my Swiss friend received the money in Swiss francs and handed it over to me. I need hardly emphasise that neither the Swiss friend nor the American firm knew that these transactions were being undertaken on behalf of the Red Army Intelligence, and I have no doubt that they would have been horrified if they had known that the Centre was in fact behind these transactions. The whole thing was regarded by these innocent intermediaries as part and parcel of the usual black bourse activities which flourished all over Europe and with a particularly virile luxuriance in Switzerland.

If I may jump ahead of my narrative a trifle and continue with financial matters, this system suited us admirably for a year or so, and a number of innocent American firms were unwitting paymasters for the network. In 1942, however, things became a trifle more difficult. By this time we had been told by the Centre that America was the only place through which we could be financed and that it was not the slightest good thinking in terms of Great Britain, Sweden, or China. (I had never seriously contemplated the proposal to use the last country. It was complicated enough trying to deal with America—the imagination boggles at the proposition of trying from Switzerland to cope adequately with the black market in Chungking.)

In 1942 the American security authorities decided that the financial arrangements for the transfer of currency abroad must be tightened up, as at that time they gave admirable loopholes through which it would be possible to finance an enemy espionage network in the United States. As a result, as a first and simple measure, it was enacted that in future banks were to inform the United States Treasury of all details regarding large cash deposits. This, not unnaturally, rather disrupted our system of financing the network as it prevented the current procedure. The Centre informed me of the new regulations and asked me to devise a new scheme. As usual they were singularly uninspired. I then delved into the dim twilight world of the local black bourse and discovered that there were a large number of individuals who had friends in America who were prepared to take the place of my well-established firms and quite certain that their relatives would not question a sudden windfall of a few thousand dollars to the credit of their relative in Switzerland. As a result I substituted individuals for firms and the whole procedure went on as merrily as before; the only difference being that instead of benefiting firms of repute, the profits of these transactions went into the pockets of the shadier members of the black-currency underworld.

The whole procedure, though simple in essence, was made immensely more complicated as I had to provide explanations to all and sundry for my desire to transfer these large sums and also the reason why I had them. It would be as tedious as it would be difficult for me to remember the variety of lies that I told to cover up these deals. I think that, on the whole, they did good, for they enhanced my reputation as an eccentric millionaire—as only a millionaire would do deals at such a ruinous rate of exchange. The rate I got was based not on the rate for a check on New York but on the rate of a dollar bill—and as any traveller abroad knows who goes to a "free market," there is the world of difference between the two. A short and cursory study today of the exchange boards of the money-changers in, for example, Tangier will show the difference.

I also had to explain how I knew that the transaction had gone through. In fact, I was of course always told by the Centre that they had paid the money into the bank in New York and I could, and did, then so inform the company or individual concerned through my Swiss friend. I naturally could not tell them I had heard over my secret transmitter that the deal was completed. As a result I used to inform them that, before the war broke out, I had envisaged such a possibility and had arranged a plain language code with my agents by which they would inform me when a deal was through. All cables were scrutinised by the Swiss and British censorships, and after Pearl Harbour by the Americans as well, so that it was out of the question to say that I had heard through normal channels. Quite often I heard from Moscow before the intermediary in Switzerland had been informed. This did not matter usually; I could laugh it off on the cover story of my plain language code. On several occasions, however, Moscow told me that the money had been paid and it proved that this statement was merely a pious hope. The Centre had told their resident director in America to do the necessary but it had not been done. In most cases this was due to pressure of work at the American end intermingled with sheer incompetence. On at least one occasion—as I learnt when I was in Moscow—the money had been embezzled by the courier, who had "gone private" with the ten thousand dollars; to my intense embarrassment as I had assured my Swiss contact—as the Centre had assured me—that the money had been paid over.

The speed of the transactions varied. Moscow told me that they could guarantee to do the whole thing from start to finish in ten days—given the requisite names. Sometimes it took a great deal less, often a great deal longer, and the longer it took the more my grey hairs grew. The financing of a Russian espionage network in wartime in the face of currency and exchange regulations was no joke, and I take a great deal of credit to myself that despite my original, pardonable ignorance of international finance and the black bourse and the lack of ideas from Moscow, I was able to keep the whole organisation solvent until my arrest.

As I have said, at this time I was seeing Rado only about twice a month in the normal course of events. It had been the original intention of the Centre to keep Rado's and my networks entirely separate once his communications were established. The idea had been that we should gradually draw apart during those spring months of 1941 and become two entirely independent organisations, as had been the position with his and Sonia's networks before the fall of France. Despite this desire on the part of the Centre to keep us apart, they had instructed Rado to arrange a place of conspiracy for me and for his principal cut-outs so that if ever anything happened to him I could step into his shoes. In point of fact the invasion of Russia put an end once and for all to any idea of separating our two organisations. The volume of traffic and the complexity of the work made it more and more imperative that we work closely in contact—and we continued to do so until the end.

In the early part of June 1942 I received instructions from the Centre to meet Rado at least twice a week and take the burden of some of the transmission work of his organisation. Rado was not a trained operator and even if he had been he had not a transmitter under his hand. From the time of receipt of information by him to its despatch over the air some twenty-four hours was liable to elapse. I, on the other hand, could encipher and send off my information in the course of one evening, as I had the set on the premises. As a result, for urgent information the Centre began to rely on me as the vehicle—though of course Rado still was the focal point for its collection.

The messages I sent to Moscow early in June had an ominous sound, and it appeared to me that if they were true the era of perpetual peace between Russia and Germany, which had been so loudly announced by Ribbentrop and Molotov less than two years ago, was rapidly coming to an end. Most of the information on this subject came from Lucy and from his source Werther in the German high command. Werther reported wholesale troop movements to the East, and unless the whole thing was an elaborate strategic bluff the information could mean only one thing—that Germany was about to unleash an attack in the East—if the information was true. At that time the Centre was deeply suspicious of Lucy. His information was regarded as too factual and too exact and Moscow suspected that the original source of it was the Abwehr, who were building up a source for use for deception purposes later. The Centre could not understand why the cut-out Taylor could not reveal the identity of his source and were constantly telling Rado to warn Taylor that the source was tainted.

Despite the Werther information and other news coming in from other sources on German troop movements, Rado himself remained firmly optimistic and refused to believe that Germany had any intention of invading Russia He thought the whole thing was part of the German "war of nerves" to obtain further political and economic advantages from the Soviet Union, and once these were obtained the whole scare would die down.

One morning toward the middle of June my telephone rang and a voice which I recognised as Rado's bade me, in the usual veiled phraseology, come to a rendezvous. When I saw Rado he was obviously worried and upset. He handed me a message which he had received from Taylor through Cissie that morning. It was from Lucy and from his source Werther. Curtly and baldly it stated that a general German attack on Russia would take place at dawn on June 22 and it gave details of the army groupings and the primary objectives. Rado could not make up his mind what to do. If the information was correct it was obviously of paramount importance that it be got off as quickly as possible. He himself inclined to the Centre's belief and thought that the whole thing was an Abwehr plant. I remember that he argued that we had not only sent the Centre intelligence of German troop movements but that Lucy had also reported what the Germans believed were Russian countermoves. These the Centre must have been in a position to evaluate and appreciate and if after so doing they continued to warn us against Lucy, then Moscow must have had cogent reasons for thinking that it was a German double-cross. I argued that it was not for us to speculate on the workings of the Centre's mind. If the information was false and we sent it, it could not do much harm—if Moscow knew it was false they would throw it into the wastepaper basket. If on the other hand it was true, it was obviously vital that the Centre should have it as soon as possible and it would be criminal for us to suppress it; far the best thing was to send it off and let the Centre do the worrying. In the end Rado agreed and handed me the message and I sent it off that night.

I learnt afterwards in Moscow that this was the first piece of Lucy's information that they did take seriously. It fitted in with information that the Russians had got from other sources and they took it into account in making their troop dispositions. For the first but not the last time Lucy had proved his worth.

The information I was sending grew increasingly ominous over the next few days, and I myself became more and more convinced that it was wishful thinking to imagine that the Germans could have put all that machinery in motion merely to frighten. I did not sleep well that Saturday night and on the Sunday morning turned my radio on early. I shall never forget hearing the hoarse voice of the Fuehrer announce the invasion of Russia. "Operation Barbarossa" was on and our real work about to start.

11

"Operation Barbarossa"

"Fascist beasts have invaded the Motherland of the working classes. You are called upon to carry out your tasks in Germany to the best of your ability. Direktor."

This was the message I received from the Centre over my radio that Sunday night. It was not a scheduled day for transmission or reception but, having spent the day listening to the strident and triumphal bellowings of the German radio, I tuned in that night to my receiving wave and at one in the morning received this message. My first from a Russia at war.

Apart from the message given above, I was also told that Moscow would be listening to me all round the clock. The whole machinery was geared to wartime production. For the next few days admonitions and instructions poured in on me from Moscow. They arranged, for the first time, a system of priorities. Messages marked "VYRDO" were exceedingly urgent and were to be decoded by the recipient at once—taking priority over all other work. "RDO" as a prefix stood for urgent and "MSG" denoted routine messages which could be transmitted and decoded at leisure. Owing to my being a one-man show, with the consequent saving of time, most of the VYRDO messages fell to my lot, and of these Lucy's material formed the major part. Gone now were the days when the Centre regarded Lucy as an *agent provocateur*. They were clamouring incessantly for more and more information—and Lucy produced it. Nearly every day new material from Werther on the grouping of the German forces which were smashing their way towards Moscow came in

98

and was sent off by me. Olga gave the organisation and strength of the Luftwaffe squadrons which were blasting the way clear for the Wehrmacht. Frequently I was so rushed that I barely had time to read the messages before encoding them and as a result did not myself digest the information they contained. If I had had the time, or if I had broken the strict rule against keeping old material, I could no doubt myself have built up the complete German order of battle in my flat in Lausanne. Time did not permit, and anyway it would have been merely of academic interest to us. The interest was far from academic to Moscow, who were virtually fighting their war on the material.

Apart from my work as an operator I was also instructed to get into contact with the Swiss Communist Party in the shape of one of its leaders, Julius Humbert Droz (cover name Droll). The Centre gave me the name of a woman, "May," who was to act as an introductory cut-out. She was an old hand in the game and had been working long before the war in, I think, another network. Her husband was an eminent and extremely respectable Zurich citizen who had no idea as to his wife's secret activities and would have been horrified had he known. I went to her extremely respectable house and introduced myself with the passwords which had been supplied by the Centre. Accepted as a Soviet agent, May arranged a secret meeting between me and Droz.

Droz was then the leader of what might be called the "right wing" of the Swiss Communist Party, with Carl Hofmeier as leader of the "left wing." Droz himself had formerly been Secretary of the Comintern and an old and trusted worker. He was also a bitter political rival of Hofmeier's. Since the outbreak of war in 1939 Hofmeier had been in contact with Rado and had received all the instructions and finances (mostly instruction; the money moved the other way) which the Centre had sent but had kept them for his own faction and refused to hand anything on to Droz, which action had not unnaturally incensed the latter, who considered that he was being slighted—having regard to his position in the past.

To my meeting with Droz I took a telegram which I had received from the Centre and which was signed by Dimitrov. I think that there is little doubt that it was in fact composed by him. The style was entirely different from that usually employed and in it Dimitrov reminded Droz of various incidents and individuals that only they two could have known—dating back to their days together in the Comintern. Dimitrov asked Droz to cooperate with me in every way and give me all the assistance he could. Armed with this letter of introduction, I went off and met Droz in the house of one of his supporters in Lausanne. He was extremely cordial to me but still angry with Hofmeier and gave me a telegram for Dimitrov complaining of the treatment meted out to him. To this I received a prompt reply, also signed Dimitrov, telling Droz that nothing could be done about it at the time as Hofmeier was rendering valuable service to the Centre. Dimitrov urged Droz to devote all his efforts to the same cause with the aid of his own supporters in the Party and hinted strongly that it was the one who did the best work for the Centre who would be confirmed in the leadership of the Party after the war.

The director authorised me to pay Droz two hundred dollars a month and reasonable expenses and also any further sums necessary for the financing of the network that Droz was to set up. This was not a difficult task for him. Among his followers were many individuals who crossed the frontier daily in the course of their normal work. With these he quickly organised a courier service which kept him in touch with local German Communists, and his followers were also able, by intelligent use of their eyes and ears, to pick up a considerable amount of information. Most of this was of local interest only but the odd scrap of military gossip or fact let slip in "careless talk" was worth sending to the Centre. Droz was also attempting to work his people into factories over the frontier so that there might later be a possibility of some serious sabotage work.

After the initial meeting it was agreed that it would be better for Droz to meet me as infrequently as possible. He was a fairly well-known person and if by chance I was observed in his company it might cause some comment. Contact was thus normally kept through May. My last (one of few) meeting with Droz nearly led to disaster.

He had asked to see me because he had an important project which he wished to discuss concerning the possible infiltration of workers into factories in Constance: not a difficult task with the frontier running through the town, but one which he thought might pay dividends. He also had some information on German troop movements in the south which he thought would be of interest. He was in a hurry and so we met in a small café run by a Party member near his home, where we could sit in the office at the back and leave separately and innocently after we had done our business. Droz left first and returned home to walk straight into the arms of the Swiss police, who were waiting for him. Luckily they had not been "tailing" him; if they had, suspicion might well have fallen on me since it was not the kind of café a foreigner would normally frequent. Droz was arrested, charged with reorganising the then illegal Swiss Communist Party—and imprisoned. As has been stated, on his release he left the Party, joined the Socialists, and is presumably now out of the net.

Droz's arrest broke up the network which had just been formed and that particular project was never revived again, but by that time the Centre had given me another task and this one contained in it the seed of disaster for the whole organisation and in the end led largely to the network's liquidation and to my own arrest.

Shortly after the invasion of Russia the Centre instructed me to get in touch with two agents of theirs with whom they had lost contact. Their names were given and the only additional information Moscow had was that they were thought to be in French Switzerland and had been for some time. These were Lorenz and Laura, in real life George and Joanna Wilmer. As I have already stated, they had worked for a long time for the Red Army abroad. Lorenz had never been a resident director but always an agent or cut-out. They were both expert in all branches of photography, from straight portraiture to document copying and microphotography, and had a well-equipped studio tucked away in a corner of their villa. When formerly in Japan they had been used only for document copying. Their sole task had been to photograph the contents of the waste-paper basket of a Japanese general high up in the Imperial General

Staff. This material was brought to them by one of the general's servants who was a secret member of the Japanese Communist Party. As neither of them knew any Japanese there was naturally a monstrous deal of chaff and very little wheat, for they photographed everything entirely unselectively. They told me that after they had been doing this for two years they heard from the Centre that one document had been so valuable that it made up for all the trouble and expense of the whole operation from its inception.

Before the war they had been working in Germany but after the outbreak of war the Centre had lost contact with them. Early in 1941 they had decided that the time had come to put themselves in touch with the Centre again. To this end they had written to an old contact of theirs, "Louis," who was still active in San Francisco as a Red Army agent (I never knew his real name), and had indicated in plain language code that they wished to get in touch with the Centre. Naturally they could not reveal their real names and address because, if Louis had been under suspicion, that would have "blown" them as well; thus they could only give the vaguest indications of their whereabouts. Hence the equal vagueness of the Centre's instructions. Presumably Louis had got in touch with his resident director, who had sent the message back to the Centre over his transmitter, and it was in turn relayed to me.

I went off to their villa, which was pleasantly situated above Lausanne, and contacted them on the pretext that I had heard that their villa was for sale. Despite the usual jargon and passwords it was with the greatest difficulty that I managed to persuade them that I was genuine and had a message for them from the Centre. They trusted me only when, very unwillingly, they had asked me to tea and I managed to show them that I knew a great deal of their past history, which I could only have learned from the Centre. After this initial coldness we became moderately friendly and I was accepted, albeit a little reluctantly, to their espionage—if not to their social—bosoms.

Lorenz claimed to be in touch with two sources of information in Germany known to the director as "Barras" and "Lambert." I never discovered anything about these two sources. Despite the fact that Lorenz asserted that they were in Germany, most of the information of a military nature that the sources produced was about troop movements and dispositions in France and the political information often had rather a French slant to it. Lorenz hinted that he had sources within the French Deuxième Bureau who had been tried and tested by him over a number of years, and I always assumed that much of his information came from these sources. The Deuxième Bureau connection should be borne in mind as it has a bearing on later events.

Despite the fact that they had been out of touch with the Centre for some years, the couple appeared to be plentifully supplied with money. Their villa was done up regardless of expense—and equally regardless of taste. Laura was, on the least provocation, swathed in mink and Lorenz was the best-dressed spy I have ever seen. They claimed to be Swiss but I am pretty certain they were Russian; they had certainly left two children in Russia last time they had been there. He was a Georgian type and faintly reminiscent of the earlier pictures of Stalin. He spoke Russian, German, and French with equal fluency, and a little English. He must have learned his French in the Midi, for it had a strong metallic tang.

Very soon I was visiting Lorenz and Laura twice weekly to gather information from their two sources—which the director appeared to value highly. Also on instructions I used Lorenz as a cut-out for various sources which were suggested from time to time by the Centre. Sometimes these sources were unknown to any of us. Instructions were merely sent that Lorenz or Laura were to go to a certain rendezvous and collect documents which would be handed over after an exchange of passwords. These were duly handed on to me and transmitted over the air to the Centre.

On one occasion Moscow suggested that it would be profitable to contact Marius Mouttet, a former French Socialist minister then a refugee in Montreux. The Centre had heard from London that Mouttet would be able to supply us with valuable political information. (This was one of the few concrete indications I ever had that the network was operating in England as well. As an abstract

speculation I have no doubt that it was—if only in a skeleton form—
but concrete indications were few as far as I was concerned.)

Lorenz duly went off and contacted Mouttet, saying he had
heard that he might help with information. Mouttet was perfectly
willing to play and offered his fullest cooperation, as he thought
Lorenz was a *British* agent. In his turn he proposed a plan to
organise the escape of Herriot from France by means of a flying
boat landing on the Lake of Geneva. Lorenz was all for going ahead
and taking information from Mouttet in the name of British intelligence. This did not seem at all a good or feasible plan as it might
have involved us in every sort and kind of international espionage
complication. If, for example, the British, who might well have received the news that Mouttet would "play" through their own
sources, contacted him and asked for his help, Lorenz's position
would have been, to say the least, a little embarrassing. Similarly
we could hardly have helped him over the flying-boat scheme. Be-
sides, I was having trouble enough financing the network as it was
organised then, and any additional financial commitments had to
be gone into with a thoroughness that a chartered accountant or
thrifty housewife might envy. If that were not enough, there was
already such a mass of information coming in that we had to edit
it down and send only the barest essentials and the cream of the
material, otherwise we would have been on the air or enciphering
the whole twenty-four hours. Thus in my capacity as espionage
housewife and blue-pencilling subeditor I asked the director's permission to drop the project—which was agreed to. Anyway I think
that Mouttet was far too wily an old fish to be "caught in the net"
and that, to continue the piscatorial metaphor, he would have soon
seen how fishy the whole thing was.

But that is enough of Lorenz and Laura for the time being. From
the time of our first contact in the late summer of 1941 until the
summer of 1943 Lorenz continued to act in most respects like a
normal Soviet agent. Not a very satisfactory one, as his reports were
verbose in the extreme and when boiled down to essentials often
contained remarkably little information, and the twenty new recruits that he put up to further his schemes were all turned down

flat by Moscow. The Centre argued, quite rightly, that money was tight enough and to take twenty new and untried sources on the pay roll was not only impossible but also flatly against the canon of Soviet espionage law.

For nearly two years, from the summer of 1941 to the summer of 1943, my life fell almost into a routine—if anything can be routine in a career where the unexpected is always coming up, and is usually dreaded. As regards the daily espionage round, late rising was an understandable rule when one was often up at all hours getting the material over to Moscow. Having breakfasted leisurely at about ten, the rest of the morning was one's own. Unless, as so often, it was one of the days to meet Rado or one of his couriers, or Lorenz at his villa, or one of the cut-outs. I tried, however, to make all these appointments in the afternoon so that I might have some time to myself and at the same time try to keep up my pose of the leisured émigré Englishman. The afternoon rendezvous were invariably tedious, as they meant a long journey to somewhere so that the contact could be on unsullied ground. Having returned, I usually had a long evening's ciphering before me. According to the rules all ciphering should have been done after dark and behind locked doors. But needs must when the Centre drove and in the more hectic times I was enciphering in all my spare moments.

My transmission time was usually about one in the morning. If conditions were good and the message short I was through in about a couple of hours. If, as frequently happened, I had long messages to send and atmospherics were bad I had to fight my way through and send when and as conditions allowed. Often on such occasions I was still at the transmitter at six and once or twice I "signed off" at nine in the morning. The nights that conditions were bad always seemed to be nights when Moscow had particularly long messages to pass back to me, which also lengthened proceedings greatly. To be on the air for that length of time broke all the normal precautions against radio monitoring. But it was a chance which had to be taken if the intelligence was to be passed over, a risk which the Centre took despite frequent admonitions by Rado and me. As regards the service intelligence, mostly Lucy's material, we were told that we must take every risk to get it over and damn the consequences. Rather cold comfort to us as we were the people who would take the consequences rather than the Centre.

In addition to the normal hazards of atmospherics the Luftwaffe added to our difficulties in getting through to Moscow. Whenever there was a German bomber raid on the Russian capital the station went off the air until the raid was over. I remember that in September and October 1941, when the Germans were hammering at the gates, we could get contact only on rare occasions and for only a short time. This got worse and worse, and on October 19 Moscow went off the air in the middle of a message. Night after night Rado and I called, and night after night there was no reply. Rado was in despair and talked of going over to the British. I was desperate as the radio silence had occurred in the middle of one of my financial deals with America and I was being pressed by my intermediaries for news and/or money—preferably the latter. Weeks passed, a month passed, and the whole delicate structure of a spy ring working at high pressure was in very real danger of disintegration. Fruitlessly we still tried every night to get contact and all we got were the derisive howls of atmospherics. Suddenly one night at the scheduled time—and six weeks after the break— the Centre piped up. As if nothing had happened, they finished the message that they had cut off halfway through, a month and a half before. Not one word of explanation or apology (not that that was expected, but a kind word would have been appreciated). When I was in Moscow I learned that this interruption had been caused by the move of the whole of the Centre's communications to Kuibishev. This move had been done at twelve hours' notice to the senior staff and none to the junior, so that the unhappy operator had been practically wrenched from his set and put in a lorry for the long trek eastward.

With such occasional alarums and excursions the months passed swiftly. As most people know, a regular and ordered life makes the time pass extremely fast and if the excitement of war is added, the whole of time seems to flow and merge in a kaleido-scopic medley. Most people I know have the greatest difficulty in sorting out exactly what they were doing at any particular moment of the war. For this reason I trust that I will be forgiven for an occasional haziness of date or blurring of recollection. Twice-weekly meetings with Rado and Lorenz, my financial deals, and the incessant grind of enciphering and transmitting occupied my life. So things went on till the crisis in the summer of 1943 which in a few months broke up the organisation and landed me in jail.

12

"SHOEMAKER'S" HOLIDAY

This chapter concerns a facet of my espionage career which does not really fit in neatly anywhere chronologically, so it must appear as an independent story on its own. The chapter heading refers to that most essential adjunct of any well-conducted spy ring—the forger. In the jargon of the Centre, a forger of passports was known as a "shoemaker" or "cobbler" and we had a very able and efficient one working for us in Switzerland.

The disadvantage of most forged passports is the very fact that they are forged. That may sound obvious but it is a very real difficulty. However good the forger may be and however complete the technical aids at his disposal, there is always the risk that some small change or some foolish mistake may land the carrier of the document in trouble. Despite the boasted efficiency of the German Secret Service and their undoubted technical ability, their forgeries during the war were often beneath contempt and were veritable death warrants to the unhappy holders. Our network avoided this difficulty completely by arranging to have our Swiss passports made by the Swiss themselves.

In the latter part of 1941 the Centre put me in touch with one Helena Schmidt (cover name "Anna") in Basle. She was an old hand, as she had been in the net for some twenty years. Before the war she had been in touch with another Soviet network which had been in existence in the country; but ever since the outbreak of war she had been out of touch with the Centre and had received no orders. I do not know exactly which network she had been working for, but suspect that it was one which had been run by the resident director who preceded Rado. Anna was a motherly old soul who looked like a superior charwoman, and I have little doubt that in the past she had acted as one. Her looks belied her; and, respectable old body as she appeared, she was deep in the network and had one most useful contact in the country. She was the cut-out between the network and a corrupt official in the Swiss Passport Office in Basle.

"Max" (I never knew his real name and in fact never met him) had also been working for the network for many years, supplying the Centre with passports for its agents. The procedure was as simple as it was easy. It would work in any country where passport office staffs are venal, and I have little doubt that it was worked by the Centre in other countries in a similar way. The Centre would supply to Max the physical details of the person for whom the passport was required. Max would then consult the files of various Basle citizens and choose a suitable identity for the new passport holder. I do not know whether he chose identities of living or dead persons, or on what principle he selected the candidate for the dubious honour of acting as *Doppelgaenger* for a Soviet spy, but it was obviously somebody who was never likely to apply for a passport himself.

This identity was then sent back to Moscow. The details naturally included date and place of birth, parentage, profession, etc., in fact all the details that are normally required for a passport in any country. The Centre then prepared a fake Swiss birth certificate. This presented little difficulty, as the invaluable Max had supplied them with the requisite forms and rubber stamps and also specimen signatures of the various registrars who had signed birth certificates over suitable years.

A completed passport application form (also of course supplied by Max) with the signature of the person requiring it in the name that Max had chosen together with his real photograph and the forged birth certificate attached were then returned to Max. He, in the normal way and in the normal course of his duties, prepared the passport and passed it for signature to the chief of police (Swiss passports are issued by the cantonal authorities). Max always took care to present the passport only when there was a large batch of them for signature and would slip the fake one in the middle of the bunch. This made it less likely that the police chief would remember who had presented the passport for signature in the improbable event of its ever being discovered to be a fake.

These false passports could of course be prolonged at any Swiss Consulate abroad. If the consular authorities were for any reason suspicious and queried it back to Basle, then the particulars, tallying in every detail, were on the passport records there. There was a gentleman's agreement between the Centre and Max that no holder of such a false passport should ever live in Switzerland on the strength of it. For his labours Max received a hundred and fifty francs a month retainer and a further hundred francs for every passport issued. Anna for her services as a cut-out received four hundred and fifty francs a month. Max was used only to supply passports. At one period the Centre instructed me to use him to obtain information, but the material that he passed to me through Anna was of no value and I did not press him on the matter, as he obviously preferred, like all good "cobblers," to stick to his last.

For the two years that I was in contact with Max the Centre never asked us to provide them with a new passport. However, one passport provided by him was due to expire in Italy. Unfortunately this one could not be renewed in the normal way as it was being used by a different agent from the one to whom it had been originally issued. As a result the signature on the renewal form would not correspond with that in the police records in Basle. The passport was brought to Switzerland through Rado's network in some way and I had it passed by Anna to Max with a request that he prolong its validity. This he did and it was returned to its owner, also via Rado.

The passport was in the name of Schneider (no connection with the Taylor of Rado's network) and I learnt later that he had been arrested and shot in Italy for espionage.

In addition to Max, Anna had another contact in the shape of her brother Hans. At the time that I rerecruited Anna into the network Hans was living in Freiburg (Germany) and like his sister was inactive. Towards the end of 1942 the director ordered me to instruct Anna to tell her brother that he would be contacted by a certain female Soviet agent, "Inge," whom the director was sending to Germany via Sweden. Also another agent would be visiting him and would hand over a short-wave transmitter, which was in turn to be handed over by Hans to Inge. This caused some difficulty to Anna as she had no secret means of communication with Hans and so had to write through the open post, giving the information in guarded language, and hope that it would escape the notice of the German censor.

Shortly afterwards I had occasion to go to see Anna again. When I got there her little flat was empty and no one knew where she had gone. I managed to contact the lawyer who had dealt with some of her affairs in the past and he told me that she had received a telegram from her brother asking her to come to Freiburg, as his wife was dangerously ill. In fact this telegram was a fake and had been sent by the Gestapo in order to lure her into Germany. After a time, as she did not turn up again, the Swiss authorities presumed that she was dead and appointed a trustee to look after her little property in Switzerland.

What had actually happened was that the radio transmitter had been found in Hans's house and he had been arrested and executed. He was known to have been in communication with Anna and I assume that the German censors passed to the Gestapo then, if not before, the cover letter from Anna to Hans. As a result the fake telegram was sent and Anna arrived in Freiburg to walk straight into the arms of the Gestapo. I learnt later in Moscow that they had questioned her without getting any result. Anna was too old a hand to talk—even under such pressure as the Gestapo could apply. In the end they threw her into a concentration camp, where she languished for the rest of the war, only to be released by the Russians when they overran it. On her release she returned to Switzerland and, for all I know, is back at her old trade. I do know that on her release the Centre paid her nothing in compensation for the years of hell that she had endured in the camp and turned her loose without a penny—not even back pay for the period of imprisonment. *Sic me servavit Apollo.*

13

The Vultures Gather

For proper understanding of the events which led to the breakup of Rado's organisation and the arrest of many of its members, it is necessary to bear the following facts and surmises in mind. As in most intelligence pictures there are some facts and many surmises; most of the facts were obtained only after I had been released from prison, and some I gathered when I was in Moscow. Without these facts in the back of the mind, many of the events of the *mouvementé* summer and autumn of 1943 appear inconsequential and illogical.

The two main antagonists to our organisation were naturally the Abwehr and the Swiss Bupo. The former because the actions of the network were aimed directly at the Third Reich and the latter because these actions were a violation of Swiss neutrality. The Abwehr were naturally the more concerned and were more active in attempting to penetrate and to liquidate the organisation. The Swiss were prepared to take action if evidence was brought to their notice but would not go out of their way to liquidate a spy network—especially if they thought it was working for the democracies. I use the word "democracies" advisedly—they became much more enthusiastic in their work when they realised it was a Soviet network, little love being lost between the bourgeois Swiss and the Soviet Union.

At some period of the war—presumably after the fall of France and before 1943—some portion of the Red Army network in Occupied Europe had been discovered by the Abwehr and the network rounded up, kept under observation, or "played back" in an endeavour to get more leads in. Either through their observations or their working of the double-cross the Germans had discovered that the network had an organisation in Switzerland. The ideal of any counterespionage organisation is to be in a position to eliminate or control an entire espionage organisation. If the former is done the enemy is rendered blind and if the latter is done he can be bemused. But in both cases it is useless to take half measures. Indeed if an attempt is being made to work a double-cross it is fatal. The portion of the network that is still working freely will at once show up that portion which is working under control, and a double-cross against the enemy which the enemy knows to be a double-cross is as dangerous as an active espionage ring. In fact more so, as you are certain that your intelligence or rather misleading intelligence is coming straight from the enemy headquarters.

In 1943 the Germans were perfectly aware that there was a Soviet spy ring operating in Swiss territory, but were unable to locate it and had no exact knowledge as to its members or its ramifications. At that time the Swiss were probably blissfully ignorant of any such thing going on in their territory, and in so far as they were interested were relying on such information as the Germans filtered through to them. The Germans would give enough information to make the Swiss take the usual police action—which would show the Abwehr exactly how far they had got—but not enough to enable the Swiss to round up the whole network—a thing the Germans preferred to do themselves.

The position of Rado's network was really similar to that of Mowgli after he had been cast out of the wolf pack. On the one hand he had the wolves—in the shape of the Bupo—who though not in active opposition were prepared if provoked to tear him to pieces, and on the other the tiger—in the shape of the Abwehr, who were really out for blood and would do anything to get the network in their power. We were assisted only by the few lone wolves, and we triumphed in the end.

I myself regard Lorenz and Laura as primary among the factors which led to the dissolution of the network. They do not, however, rank in the tiger category. Nothing better than jackals is worthy of them if my beliefs are correct.

My suspicions of Lorenz really began towards the end of 1942. By that time I had been in contact with him long enough and felt that he was quite out of the ordinary as regards Soviet spies. After one has dealt with secret agents in all walks of life one begins to have a feeling regarding them and their genuineness—and this I never had towards Lorenz and Laura. They were both far too mondaine, and she was far too chic to be part of a Red Army net. Also the information that they produced was not in any way high-grade— despite the golden opinions the director had about their capabilities. Their mode of life, their actions, their information, and the whole appearance of the setup filled me with a vague sense of uneasiness. Facts—or rather suspicions on my part made the whole affair more sinister.

As is known to the veriest tyro in Soviet espionage it is strictly forbidden for any agent to know, or to attempt to find out, the name of his contact. This is laid down for the mutual protection of both parties in case one or the other is caught. It is nothing but clear, practical common sense. Lorenz, however, did not subscribe to this. As I have said, shortness of time and pressure of work prevented me from obeying the rules in their strictest sense—and as a result I used to meet Lorenz in his villa. This procedure was accepted with alacrity by him as he alleged that it was difficult for him to get out and anyway the seclusion of the villa, tucked away in the foothills round the lake, made it an admirable conspiratorial rendezvous. That should have been enough; the rules had already been broken sufficiently without any further violation of elementary security. Despite this Lorenz showed a persistent desire to discover my name, or, if that were impossible, at least some sort of clue as to where I lived and my mode of life. Idle curiosity, it may be thought; I thought so at the time, but now I am inclined to think rather differently.

Lorenz tried to gratify his curiosity in a number of ingenious ways. Every time I went to visit him, though he knew that my time was precious, he insisted that I take off my overcoat and leave it in his extremely nicely furnished hall. While I was urged into the lounge, just off the hall on the left of the front door, by Lorenz, Laura would be, allegedly, getting the information that they had collected from their secret hiding place. This procedure appeared perfectly logical to me the first few times I visited them—even though the procedure was time-wasting and tedious for me. Unfortunately for all concerned, I was, and am, a martyr to the cigarette habit and an inveterate chain smoker. One day—it must have been in the late autumn of 1942—I went round to the villa to pick up their material and, having succumbed to the usual pressure, had gone into the lounge for the usual drink. On arrival there I found that my pockets were empty and that I had left my packet of cigarettes in my overcoat. I moved in a purposeful manner towards the door and was prevented almost by force by Lorenz from trying to get into the hall. Lorenz offered me one of his atrocious cigarettes with a rather feeble excuse. This I refused to smoke; with some justification as Lorenz smoked some vile brand. An embarrassed pause ensued with Lorenz firmly holding the door and after a moment he offered me a cigar which I accepted and he retired, allegedly to his cigar cabinet, to find it—it never appeared. After a short period Laura appeared, rather flushed, and the party went on as before.

Not being of a naturally suspicious nature, it took some time for the full significance of this incident to dawn on me anyway, at least as long as it took to go by tram from their villa back to the corner near my flat. I then mulled the whole thing over in my mind and decided that I would see whether it was the result of an overheated mind or whether there was perhaps some undercurrent going on which the Centre might regard with some disfavour. I was not in the least bothered as to what anyone might find in any of my pockets. By that time I was a comparatively old bird in the espionage field and had had made for me a couple of detachable pockets which hung down inside the front of my trousers and attached to the front brace buttons. When full they gave me a rather middle-aged spread but I was prepared to sacrifice my vanity to security. The pockets would not have stood up to any sort of trained search but they did provide complete security against casual prying. Even Laura could hardly have got away with my trousers—though she did her best with my coat. In these pockets I kept all my personal papers such as my passport and *permis de séjour*—made out of course in my right name. There also I used to carry my gun, save in times of emergency when I used to extract it from its hiding place: a small .32 automatic, it gave me moral comfort at some of my more difficult rendezvous. Taking a tip from the films, I used, on such occasions as I thought I might have to use it and yet might be liable to search, to hide it in my hat, where it rested conveniently, if not comfortably, on the crown of my head.

Being a little chary of Laura's rather Fagin-like habits over my pockets, I naturally made things as easy for her as possible, and on my subsequent visits to the villa filled my pockets with purely innocuous documents, in a certain order and with certain papers interleaved, with the result that I was quite certain that the couple were, for whatever obscure purpose of their own, doing their best to find out what they could about me.

Any spy gets morbidly suspicious, but I do not think my suspicions of Lorenz and Laura were unjustified. They had done their best to discover my personal particulars by searching my pockets—hardly what is expected of a friendly spy; they had also done their best to discover where I lived—in this they were not successful until much later on, which is another story. Apart from this they were obviously living at a rate and in a style which even the Centre at its most expensive would hardly have sanctioned. They had also been living in Lausanne for some time before the war and had not taken the trouble to inform the Centre of the fact and had not started to get in touch again until 1941. Their villa in itself must have cost some six thousand pounds, and it would have been impossible to get this sum of money together from the Centre honestly. Also the villa and property were in Laura's name which gave the whole thing a slightly more shady air.

I communicated my suspicions, as best I could, to the director and requested that, owing to my feelings of disquiet, I should be allowed to maintain contact with the couple through a cut-out—

thus obviating any possibility that they might discover the real identity of their contact, which they had been trying to do so assiduously for the past months. In reply I received what can only be described as a "rocket" from Moscow. I remember the message well, because it came over to me in the spring of 1943 when my fears about Lorenz were at their height. As soon as I started decoding I realised from the reference number that the Centre was referring to my signal full of doubts and fears—and full of doubts and fears I decoded the answer, which did little to increase my peace of mind.

The director informed me that I was entirely mistaken and hinted strongly that I was suffering from "outstation suspicions" (a convenient phrase to cover any deficiency by the Moscow section concerned). He added that both Lorenz and Laura had worked faithfully over a long period of years and that their information was regarded as vital. I was told that it was essential that I maintain personal contact with them as only in that way could it be ensured that their information reached Moscow early. I was not impressed by this. By no stretch of imagination could their information even begin to compare with that produced by Lucy, and anyway most of it struck me as turgid, verbose, and unimportant in the extreme. However, the orders of the Centre were the orders of the Centre and as a result I continued to have contact with them until one particularly blatant incident which caused me to sever contact with this couple once and forever.

It was in the early summer of 1943 that Lorenz and Laura made their last attempt to discover my identity. Normally I visited their villa in the late evening (as I have stated, they refused to rendez-vous elsewhere) because I hoped that in the dusk my visits were less likely to be observed. On this occasion, however, I received a message that Lorenz wished to see me urgently; that the evening would not do and I must come up to his villa at lunchtime. It was a broiling day, one of those days when one wishes passionately to be out of all this intrigue, to go and walk in the cool hills. I toiled laboriously up to the villa, cursing the day I was born and the fact that I had ever succumbed to the bait hung out to me in London. Espionage is not good for one's condition; in fact it might be called sweated labour if long hours in an enclosed atmosphere are criteria.

Lorenz greeted me warmly on my arrival and took me into the lounge, which was curtained and shuttered and as a result stiflingly hot. This Lorenz airily explained away as a precaution against eavesdropping. He handed me a long message which he stated was the most important information Lambert and Barras had produced to date. It dealt with troop movements and contained a certain amount of military information which, if true, would have been of some importance. It was, however, of immense length and extremely verbosely written. In the course of a long interview I went over it with Lorenz and attempted to cut it down into manageable length. After a few minutes of this, in the Turkish-bathlike atmosphere of the lounge, I was dripping with sweat and on Lorenz's urging I removed my coat.

After we had dealt with the message as best we could Lorenz suggested a turn in the garden and we went out through the long French windows onto the lawn. As we stepped out Lorenz "absent-mindedly" closed the window, which was fitted with a self-locking Yale lock, with the result that we were locked out and had, after our stroll, to go round to the front of the house and ring the front doorbell—which was opened by Laura after a long delay. I was quite certain that this was yet another attempt to discover my identity by going through my coat pockets, which they thought might yield more profitable dividends than my overcoat. Of course these efforts were abortive as everything was still in the "pouch" pockets in the front of my trousers. I was busy congratulating myself on having avoided the trap, but was that moment stepping into yet another neatly contrived one. The front door was set at an angle to the front of the building and as I stood outside the door with Lorenz waiting for Laura to open the door she was busy photographing me through a hole in the shutter. This of course I did not know at the time and only learnt it when I was in Moscow. The Russians had discovered the whole story from captured German documents.

What in fact had happened was that Lorenz and Laura had gone over to the Germans some time before, probably before the war.

Their handsome villa and expensive mode of life was made possible by Abwehr finance. The information that they had been supplying had been in its turn supplied by the O.K.W. and was a clever mixture of truth and fiction. Most of the truth consisted of unimportant facts which there could be no harm in the Russians knowing, or facts concerning troop movements, etc., which could be of no use to the Russians as they would not affect the eastern front. The information they had given me that evening was false and was designed to affect the course of a battle being fought at that time.

On looking back at it all afterwards I realised that it had once been suggested, indirectly, that I also should work for the Germans. It was at a dinner party at the villa. The service, food, and silver were well up to the standard of luxury of the rest of the place. I congratulated Lorenz on having such pleasant things and he told me that if I liked I, too, could be in a similar position. He had been at Leningrad University with the head of the Russian Counterespionage Department and naturally as a result he had the complete confidence of Moscow. He suggested that I should suggest to Moscow that I work under him and hand over the communications network to him. In return he, Lorenz, would guarantee me five hundred dollars a month and five hundred dollars' expenses over and above what I was getting at that time and in addition would have no work to do as Lorenz would do it all for me and I could lead a life of leisure allegedly "talent-spotting" for the network. I passed Lorenz's statements on verbatim to Moscow and added that I did not like the idea at all. The Centre told me to tell Lorenz that they would have nothing to do with it and added that it would be useless anyway as I knew the code and would still be able to check up on Lorenz's material and that they had no intention of sending out another code to the Swiss network.

It is obvious what Lorenz, or rather his German masters, wanted. With me out of the way and the code in their hands they could not only pick up the remainder of the network at their leisure but also use the channel for deception purposes if they wished. The Centre had prevented that plan from working, and so the Germans had to fall back on identifying me and then abducting me so that they could extract the necessary information from me by torture.

The Abwehr are nothing if not efficient and they put two operations in hand—both of which were successful. One was probably planned in Paris and the other in Switzerland and it was thanks to this separate planning that, though successful in their primary aim, that of identifying me, they were not successful in their ultimate aim, that of getting me into their power.

Early in June I received instructions from the Centre to meet a courier from France and hand over some money to him for the French network. I was given four different days as rendezvous. The first two inside the entrance of the funicular station at Ouchy, and the last two inside the main entrance of the Botanical Gardens at Geneva. All meetings were to be at midday and I was given the necessary passwords and control questions and also descriptions as to how both the courier and I were to be dressed. No one contacted me on the first three days and it was only at the last rendezvous, the second time I was at the Botanical Gardens, that an individual came up to me and we exchanged the correct passwords and I handed over the money.

The director had ordered me to have no conversation with the courier but merely to hand over the cash and go away. However, the courier handed over to me in his turn a large book done up in a bright orange paper and told me that between two of the pages I should find three ciphered messages which must be sent off urgently by radio to the Centre. He also said that he had valuable information which he wanted to get over and suggested a further meeting as soon as possible and named a place near Geneva—which was also very near the German-controlled French frontier.

All this made me very suspicious as such loquacity against strict orders was unusual in a Soviet agent. I began to suspect that perhaps the original courier had been arrested and his place taken by an Abwehr agent. The orange wrapping would serve as a convenient beacon light for anyone who was trailing me home, and the meeting place near the frontier would serve admirably for an abduction in the best Gestapo traditions. As for the cipher messages—

if these were also phony, then they would serve as admirable pointers towards identifying my transmitter. I had no doubt that the Germans had long been monitoring the network and if on one of the services that they were listening to they suddenly found the three messages they had planted it would at once identify that transmitter as mine.

I tried to dissemble my suspicions as much as I could and said that I could not attend a meeting that week as I had business elsewhere and so fixed on a meeting in a week's time. On leaving the rendezvous I hid the book as well as I could under my coat and returned home by a roundabout route, taking evasive action. In my next transmission I reported on this fully to the director and he agreed that I should not attend the meeting. As regarded the cipher messages, which were there as the courier had said, gummed between two pages and in a cipher that I did not know, the director asked me to send them over but so to disguise them with dummy groups and then by re-enciphering in my own cipher, that they would neither be recognisable as the original messages to the monitors nor serve as a guide to our cipher to the cryptographers.

A fortnight later the Centre informed me that my suspicions were correct and that the courier had been a German agent and that as I had been recognised by at least one member of the Abwehr I must regard myself in jeopardy and at least partially compromised. I was therefore to break all connection with Rado and his group and contact my own agents only through a system of cut-outs. I took this opportunity to break finally with Lorenz and Laura and told Moscow that this was because they had refused to deal with me through a cut-out. This was probably lucky for me as I learnt afterwards in Moscow that the Russians had discovered from captured German documents that I was to be kidnapped at my next rendezvous with Lorenz and taken to Germany.

From the end of June 1943 I had contact with Moscow only about twice a week, and the traffic was principally concerned with financial transactions and reporting on the liquidation of Anna and her group. As regarded finance, it was about this time that I started my most ambitious single financial transaction. I was arranging for the transfer of a hundred thousand dollars from the United States for our use in Switzerland. The innocent intermediary in this case was a Swiss firm with, of course, a branch in New York. The Centre was being more than usually tiresome and insisting that the money should be paid in ten separate installments of ten thousand dollars each, while the Swiss company wanted it in a lump sum. The negotiations dragged on for months and it was not till the end of October that a compromise was finally reached whereby the money was to be paid in two equal sums of fifty thousand dollars each. In order to see fair play it had been arranged that the Swiss franc equivalent of this sum, three hundred thousand francs at the black market rate, should be paid into an account in the names of two lawyers, one to be nominated by each side. I approached a well-known Lausanne lawyer, known to me only by reputation, and asked if he would act for me, explaining that it was a normal business black market transaction. Unfortunately for me my arrest came just before the transfer could be made; this was, however, fortunate for the lawyer as otherwise he might have found himself in the embarrassing position of being the unwitting paymaster of a Russian spy.

After I had reported on the arrest of Anna and completed the preliminaries for the transfer of the hundred thousand dollars I had little to do, as I was now out of touch with Rado on Moscow's orders. As a result I got permission from the Centre to take a holiday and so in September I had a well-earned rest in Tessin, far away from the hurly-burly, excitement, and fatigue of international espionage.

In my absence, however, that precious pair, Lorenz and Laura, had not been idle. On my return I questioned my concierge Madame Muller as to whether anyone had been inquiring for me in my absence. She then told me that a couple, answering to the description of Lorenz and Laura, had been round and had tried to pump her as to my friends and my habits. The excuse that they gave was not uningenious. Laura said she was very worried as I had been at one time very much in love with her sister and had indeed not only promised to marry her but things had gone so far that it was imperative that I should marry her. However, at this stage my affections had apparently cooled off and they were trying to find out whether there was not perhaps another attraction which had seduced me from the charms of her sister. If there was someone, then they wished to contact them and warn them of my "true character" as a heartless seducer. They had also visited my charwoman, Hélène, with a similar story, and had offered money to both in an endeavour to extract the information.

They were, however, singularly unsuccessful. The life of a Soviet agent leaves little time for romance. My day was far too full with contacting my sources, coding, decoding, and transmitting, for me to have any time for amorous dalliance. Any spare time I had I spent in a vain attempt to catch up on my arrears of sleep. I was also not such a fool as to meet my contacts in my flat, so that this little effort was almost useless from Lorenz's, or rather the Abwehr's, point of view. Not quite, however, as they obviously now knew my address and name as well as having my photograph.

Previously Lorenz had made one other effort to get me out of the way. After my arrest I learnt that the Swiss police had received a denunciation from the French Consulate General in July. The denunciation, as my name was then unknown to Lorenz, merely consisted of my photograph with a statement that the original of the photograph was an important Soviet spy who was working a radio transmitter from Lausanne. The police took no notice of this as they received hundreds of such denunciations each day, and it was only later that they connected this up with Rado and his network. This denunciation had obviously come from Lorenz, since only he had my photograph and he also had good connections with the French Deuxième Bureau. The reason why Lorenz was anxious for me to be arrested by the Swiss, and only in the last resort by the Germans, was obvious. It arose from no nice feelings about shedding blood, but from a very lively sense of self-preservation. Not only was he being financed by the Abwehr but also he had been receiving large sums of money from me none of which he had thought fit to declare to the Germans. Also he knew that if I were arrested I could give a fairly complete picture of his past (which I had learnt from Moscow before I first contacted him), which details he was not anxious for the Germans to know. Over and above this he was living in Switzerland on Swiss papers and wished to go on living there after the war—a war which at that time he could see it was unlikely that Germany would win. It was therefore in his interest to keep his hands as clean as possible and get me safely shut up in a Swiss prison where I could do him no harm; but this must be arranged in such a way that he was kept out of it, or there might be awkward questions as to how exactly he knew all the facts. Hence the anonymous denunciation via the French.

After these efforts in the summer of 1943 Lorenz and Laura faded out of the story. I ascertained after my release that they were still living in their villa and for all I know may still be doing so. When in Moscow I was told that an N.K.V.D. man was being sent to Switzerland who would have, *inter alia*, the task of interviewing them. I can only hope that they enjoyed it and are still in a position to enjoy their handsome villa and their luxurious mode of life. I somehow think it unlikely that they are still in the net in the espionage sense of the word. If they returned to Russia the net would be more likely to have a literal rather than literary connotation with a strong flavour of labour camp about it.

I informed Moscow of this visit by Lorenz and Laura, and they replied that I must at once move and set up somewhere else in Switzerland. Easier said than done, as at that time I was again in constant radio touch with the Centre and to find another place and to get police permission to move there would take a very long time.

The reason for my daily contact with the Centre was that I was ordered to renew my contact with Rado. He also had been having Abwehr trouble and was anticipating more. In his case it had been partially sheer bad luck. One day in a restaurant he had come face to face with a former Soviet agent who before the war had gone over to the Germans. The agent recognised him and after this Rado believed that he was being watched by the Abwehr. He said that he thought that Margarete Bolli, ("Rosie") was being watched also, and he had therefore taken her transmitter away for the moment. He gave no reason for Rosie's having fallen under suspicion and it was only later that I learnt that he had been committing one of the major espionage sins of mixing business with pleasure and had been having an affair with Rosie and that she had been in the restaurant with him when he was spotted.

Another cause for disquiet was that, during the time I had severed contact with Rado, two persons had gone to see Cissie (Rachel Duebendorfer, one of Rado's principal cut-outs), stating that they came from me, and had given both my real and my cover name, Jim. The latter meant nothing to Cissie as she did not know it and anyway we had never met—though we knew of each other's existence. She refused to have anything to do with them and stated that she had never heard of anybody called Foote, and "Jim" conveyed less than nothing to her. I can only assume that this was yet another attempt by the Abwehr to get into the network. Cissie was an old hand at the game, so they may have got her name as a result of interrogations of other captured agents elsewhere.

The Abwehr were not slow to take advantage of the lead given them by the accidental encounter of the traitor Soviet spy with Rado. They decided that Rosie was probably easier game and so concentrated their efforts on her. A handsome blond Aryan Abwehr agent, one Hans Peters, was put on the job. He managed "accidentally" to scrape an acquaintance with the girl and the acquaintance quickly ripened into friendship and more. Time lay heavy on her hands during the day, as she had nothing to do save transmit several nights a week, so she was not averse to having an attentive youth at her beck and call. He was able to take her out and give her a good time; and the Abwehr were not averse to paying for it.

In view of the recognition of Rado and the Cissie incident, Rado and I agreed to limit our contact to the minimum and meet only under cover of darkness. He also contacted the Swiss Communist Party and asked them to have hiding places ready for us if it became necessary for the organisation to go underground. From this time, the end of September, things moved swiftly forward to a crisis.

14

THE 'DOCTORS' DECIDE

The position then, at the end of September 1943, in the "cold war" between the Abwehr and ourselves showed a marked improvement in the Abwehr's score. They had made appreciable progress in their investigations into the network. They knew my name and address and that I was running a network and a transmitter in Lausanne. They knew Rado's name and address and had an agent well in with one of his organisation. They knew that Cissie had something to do with the network. They did not know of any connection between Rado and me.

So far emphasis has been laid on German activities against us and little or nothing has been said as regards the Swiss, who after all were somewhat concerned, because though the organisation was not directed against Swiss interests we were to some extent abusing Swiss hospitality by our activities. Also, as a last resort, if kidnapping and strong-arm methods failed, the Abwehr could always tip off the Swiss and have us arrested by the Bupo, which would at least liquidate a portion of the network. This was not, however, necessary, as the Swiss had not been inactive.

The Swiss had an efficient monitoring system and it subsequently transpired that they, like the Germans, had been monitoring our traffic for some time. Their original information, however, came from a casual source or so I was told by the Swiss police after my arrest.

At some time, it must have been a year or so previously, one of the wireless staff at the Geneva airport had been casually twiddling the tuning dial of his set. No planes were due in and he had no signals to listen to and was looking for something on the short wave with which to lighten his boredom. Suddenly he picked up a strong signal transmitting in Morse but in code and using amateur procedure. This intrigued him as all amateur radio transmissions had been forbidden in Switzerland since the outbreak of war, and anyway an amateur transmitting five-figure groups was somewhat more than unusual. He noted the call sign and frequency and reported the matter to his superiors, and the report finally filtered through to the Bupo and the army.

The station was monitored and in due course by D.F. they discovered that it was located in Geneva. In the course of their investigations they came across another set, also working from the town and using a similar procedure. These sets were, of course, those of Bolli and Hamel. At that time the Swiss police were under the impression that these were either British transmissions or possibly a local Communist network working into Germany. It seems likely that at the same time they also picked up my transmissions from Lausanne and monitored them as well.

Exactly why the Swiss took no action for a period of at least a year, and only started offensive action against these sets in the autumn of 1943, I do not know. It is possible that they were hoping to get enough traffic to enable them to break the cipher, or it may be that they were unwilling to take action against sets which they thought were being worked by the Allies. Indeed they might never have taken action against them unless pressure had been brought to bear by the Abwehr, who could and may have given them the facts. The only people who can answer that question are the Swiss police and the Swiss General Staff. The fact remains that it was not till the autumn that any serious action was taken—and this speedily proved successful.

Mobile D.F. vans were ordered into action but it was not easy to locate the exact whereabouts of the two Geneva transmitters, as they were in a built-up area (which was the precise reason why they had been put there by us). When the vans had pinpointed the two transmitters to a comparatively small area, another technique was brought into play, one which was originated, I believe, by the

Germans and used with much success to locate Allied transmitters working in occupied countries. During the time that the sets were on the air they cut off the current from each house in succession. When on pulling the switch the set went off the air they were certain that they had identified the house in which it was located. This they did, in turn, with both Bolli's and Hamel's transmitters.

On October 9 I was sitting in a café drinking my morning cup of coffee when I saw in the first edition of the *Tribune de Genève* a small announcement that a secret short-wave transmitter had been discovered in Geneva and its operators arrested. This item was removed from all subsequent editions of the paper and it was mere chance that it caught my eye. That night I heard the Centre vainly calling the Hamel transmitter, and feared the worst. The next morning my telephone rang and I heard Rado's voice at the other end. "You will be sorry to hear that Edward is much worse and the doctor has been called in. He decided after consultation that the only thing to do was to take him to hospital." I made suitable sympathetic noises to keep up the pretence, but my mind was working furiously. This meant that the only firm link with the Centre was my transmitter, with the possible doubtful use to which we might put Bolli's (here I was overoptimistic). Rado's agitation, though suitable to the tenor of the conversation, was also perfectly genuine. With the "doctor" looking after Hamel, Rado felt the "hospital" looming unpleasantly near for him also.

A day or so later he telephoned me again and said that he was coming over to see me in my flat under cover of darkness, a thing he had never done before and an action symptomatic of his agitation. He arrived and told me that not only had the Hamels been arrested but the police had also simultaneously raided Margarete Bolli's flat and arrested her as well. Hamel had been caught *flagrante delicto*, sitting working the transmitter; Margarete had been caught equally in the act but in rather a different sense as she had been found in bed with Peters, the Abwehr agent, who had succeeded only too admirably in his task of getting into the girl's confidence. A complication, slightly embarrassing to the Abwehr, was that Peters had been arrested also as an accomplice!

We never understood why the Swiss, having held their hands so long, acted in the end with such precipitancy. They had not kept the buildings under observation; but if they had they could have scooped the whole gang, including Rado. As it was, Rado had a narrow escape as he went round to see Hamel a few hours after his arrest and while the police were still searching the flat. Luckily he happened to glance at a clock which Hamel kept in his shop-window and the hands showed danger. It had been agreed that the hands of the clock should show midday when all was clear. During transmission times or if danger threatened the hands were changed to some other time. As Hamel was transmitting at the time of his arrest the signal showed danger, and Rado was warned before he knocked and fell into the hands of the police.

All this was reported to the Centre over my set—which was now the only link the network had with Moscow. The director expressed concern, but stated that Lucy's information was so important that we must continue working despite the arrests, and he ordered Rado and me to make every effort, with the aid of the local Party, to recruit new operators and construct new sets.

Rado was frantic with worry and anxiety—worry over the breakdown of the organisation and anxiety concerning his personal safety. He had cause for anxiety, for he had broken practically every security precaution in the espionage code. Fearing that he was being tailed, he had, some time previously, deposited all his records with Hamel, who had a secure hiding place built into his flat. These records contained not only all the financial details of the network but also copies of telegrams which had been sent, often with the encoded version attached to them. As if this were not sufficient, he had also been idiotic enough to leave a copy of his code book there, and this, too, fell into the hands of the police. He feared, not without reason, that his code was compromised and that, with the material captured, the Swiss would be able to read all the back traffic that he had sent, which they had picked up through their monitoring of the sets. This meant that not only was I the only physical link with the Centre but also that my code was the only one which could be used.

The police haul had been even better than this. Among the messages that they discovered was one giving the details of a new Swiss Oerlikon cannon which was still on the secret list, and from the messages the Swiss were able after some study to discover that the source of much of the military information was none other than their trusted military evaluator, Lucy himself. Thus not only was Rado guilty of espionage against Swiss interests, which would make the Bupo doubly anxious to get to the bottom of the affair, but his ill-considered actions had imperilled our most valuable source as well. I also shrewdly suspected that, among the other miscellaneous financial papers, the police would find clear pointers towards me and the rest of the network. My fears were not ungrounded as subsequent events showed.

A few days later Rado reported that the Geneva Communist Party had been able to make contact with the Hamels and Bolli through the agency of a prison warder who was a secret member of the Party. Hamel told us that he had been shown a photograph of me and told that the original was the head of the entire network. They did not know then of the existence of Rado—or so it appeared. (The photograph of course was the one supplied by Lorenz.)

Rado had gone to ground in Berne, but soon after he plucked up courage and went back and lived openly at his flat. He noticed, however, that it was under observation, or he thought it was, and went to ground again in the flat of a couple of Party sympathisers in Geneva.

All this was reported back to the Centre, who ordered me to take control of the entire group, and the director stated that he had given orders to Rado to put me in touch with his two main cut-outs, Pakbo and Cissie. Although Rado had now ceased to use his cipher, the Centre still sent occasional messages in it for him. They regarded their codes as unbreakable unless the key fell into the wrong hands and could not believe that an old hand like Rado had been so foolish as to hand the whole thing to the Swiss on a plate—as he had done.

Rado agreed to put me in touch with Pakbo, but said that Cissie declined to have any contact with me. He said that owing to the visit of the two presumed German agents to her flat a month or two back she feared that she would be compromised if she was in direct touch with me. That was Rado's story; but I learnt after my release that it bore little relation to the truth. In fact, Cissie had asked to be put in touch with me but this Rado had refused to do. The reasons were not difficult to understand. Rado wished at all costs to keep control of the organisation and in order so to do was prepared to disobey the director's orders. He also knew that it would be extremely embarrassing to him were I to meet Cissie and compare notes—especially on finance. Rado had been indenting on me for large sums of money to pay Cissie and her agents but had been keeping a large proportion of this money for himself. This discrepancy would immediately come out when we met—as it did a year later.

As a result Rado stated that he would continue to receive the Lucy information through Cissie and pass it on to me through a cut-out. He also said that he would act as cut-out between Jean Beauchamp and me. Jean was the son of a Communist leader and was busy recruiting wireless operators for the time when we could once again start up new sets. We also arranged for a place of conspiracy for Jean and me in case of emergency.

Rado therefore suggested that the best thing for the network and himself would be for him to take refuge in the British Legation (there was, of course, no Soviet representation in Switzerland and the nearest Soviet official was in Ankara or London). Once there, with him safely inside the hedge of diplomatic immunity, the network could continue functioning as before—with the one difference that the British would have to be brought into the picture. Rado himself was not in touch with the British but Pakbo, through his cut-out Salter, the Balkan service attaché, made the approach and Rado received the reply that the British were prepared to harbour him if necessary. The Swiss end of the deal was therefore settled and he had only to square the Centre. I therefore passed on to the Centre Rado's request that he should be allowed to retire from the world and take refuge with the British. Almost by return transmission I received a most emphatic "No." The Centre added that they could not understand how such an old hand as Rado could even think of making such a suggestion, as "the British would track down his lines of communication and use them for themselves."

This idea of Allied cooperation rather shook Rado, but it was not in the least inconsistent with the attitude that the Centre had adopted on previous occasions. Once, in 1942, Rado had had in his hands certain documents and plans which would have been of great value to the British as well as to the Russians, but the material was so bulky that it was impossible for us to pass it over the air. He therefore had suggested that it be handed over to the Allies—through a suitable and secure cut-out of course. The Centre's reaction was immediate. Rado received instructions to burn the information at once. From the director's point of view there was little difference between information falling into German or British hands. It was Russian information and if it could not be passed to the Centre, then the right place for it was the wastepaper basket—however valuable it might be to Russia's allies.

In the meantime I received further news from Hamel through the "fellow-travelling" warder in the jail. Hamel had been told by his interrogators that there was another transmitter working in Lausanne and that a posse of army technicians had been sent out to track it down.

I informed the Centre of this and was told that Lucy's information was still so vital that I must risk everything and continue to transmit. In the meantime, until other transmitters were available and I was able to move my residence, I was to send no information at all save for Lucy's material.

At this time I was seeing Rado twice weekly—or as near as we could make it, having regard to his fears and to my other appointments. The only point of these meetings was for Rado to pass on Lucy's material and any messages he might have about the reconstruction of the network. At our rendezvous we used to check up carefully to see whether we were being followed and this paid good dividends. On one occasion towards the end of October we had arranged to meet just inside the Parc d'Eaux Vives in Geneva. Rado arrived by taxi and entered the park. I noticed that the driver of the cab, as soon as he had been paid, drove off but stopped almost at once at a telephone kiosk into which he hurriedly shut himself. I told Rado and we decided at once that, trivial as the incident might be, we had better play for safety and we left the park at once by separate gates. We went just in time. I learnt later that the police had circulated a photograph of Rado to all cab drivers in Geneva. The driver in question had recognised his fare and rung up police headquarters. A hurry call had been sent out to the various squad cars prowling round the town and they covered all the exits. But they were too late, for Rado and I had left and arranged a somewhat less disturbed rendezvous elsewhere.

This little incident put the finishing touch to Rado's fears. From that time on it was impossible to lure him out of his hidey-hole with the local Communist Party. In fact he remained underground until he left the country a year later, and took virtually no further part in the network. His nerve had been going for some time. Small blame to him as he had been working under a strain for many years. This strain had been increased by the fortuitous addition, through the accident of war, of a number of other networks to his own. He had coped manfully with the dribs and drabs of heterogeneous networks thrown at his head and succeeded up to a point and for some time. I prefer to remember him at the height of his power as the genial cartographer to the world at large, and the successful spymaster to the favoured few, rather than as the hunted rat of his last Swiss days or the frightened, broken man of Paris and Cairo. Only the Centre knows his fate. He certainly cheated many out of their just dues, but equally he drove them to obtain the best results. He had been faithful to his masters after his fashion.

To make matters worse, at that time the network was very short of money. Our cash reserves were down to five thousand dollars. Rado himself was completely broke and in addition had borrowed five thousand dollars from the local Communist Party and a further five thousand from Pakbo. At that time the network was costing some ten thousand dollars a month in salaries and expenses alone—quite apart from extras such as bonuses. To make financial matters worse, the director had authorised me to spend ten thousand dollars to finance a plan for the escape of the Hamels and Bolli from prison. This sum was needed as a bribe to the "fellow-traveller" warder and his colleagues. The director set great store by this plan as he was apprehensive lest Bolli, the least experienced of the three, should break down under interrogation. She knew Pakbo's and my real names and, of course, a great deal about Rado. The Hamels were not so important as they knew the names of none of the network save that of Jean Beauchamp, who had recruited them, though they knew Rado and me by sight.

I need not have worried unduly about the financial side, as matters were swiftly taken out of my hands. On the night of November 19/20 I contacted Moscow at the scheduled time, which was then half past midnight. I passed over a short message to them and then began taking down a long message which they had for me.

Three quarters of an hour later there was a splintering crash and my room was filled with police. At one-fifteen in the morning of November 20 the "doctors" took the matter into their own hands. I was arrested and the last link between the Centre and Switzerland was broken.

15

"HOSPITAL" AND AFTER

The arrest did not go quite according to plan, and as a result I was able to save something from the wreck. The door was meant to give at once under the axe and fly open so that I could be caught in the act. In fact the lock did not give and it was the doorframe itself which went. As a result there were about three minutes while the police were prising their way in, which breathing space I put to good use. I managed to put my set out of commission and burn the few documents I had in a large brass ash tray which I kept handy for the purpose. The conflagration was helped by the judicious addition of lighter fuel from a handy bottle also kept for just such an emergency.

My first reaction to this somewhat unceremonious entry was that it was the Abwehr who had arrived, and the notion was not dispelled by the first remark made by the uniformed figures who poured in. A voice shouted *"Hände Hoch!"*, and the comment was emphasised by a most pointed demonstration with an automatic pistol. A second glance reassured me that I was still in the hands of the democracies.

The police were accompanied by two radio technicians who attempted at once to continue radio communication but they could do nothing with my damaged transmitter. There was also present a genial bearded young cryptographer, Marc Payot, who made a fruitless search for clues to help him break the cipher. He confessed to me later, when he came to see me in prison, that he had worked on the cipher for months with no result. His initial mistake was in assuming that it was similar in type to Rado's—which of course he could now read thanks to Rado's carelessness. I learned later in Moscow that the technicians had attempted to continue communication with the Centre and a day or so later called up Moscow on my set, which they had then managed to repair. My call signs they of course knew, as they had been monitoring my traffic for months, but they made the mistake of using Rado's code—the only one they had. This at once aroused the suspicions of the Centre, who began to smell a rat, and the Moscow operators also recognised that there was a difference in transmission technique. A few trick questions from the director soon showed him that the set was being worked by the Swiss and that they were not being helped by any of the network.

While Inspectors Pasche and Knecht, who were in charge of the raid, searched the flat, I was taken out into the hall and put under the guard of a young armed detective. I began rather smugly to congratulate myself that I had left no clues behind, for I had been expecting some sort of action for weeks, ever since the first arrests, and had destroyed all my records, cash accounts, etc., and as a result there was nothing for the police save a heap of charred ashes and a damaged transmitter. My pleasant daydream was rudely shattered when I saw lying on the hall table my electric torch. It was one of the long thin type which take two 1½-volt batteries. The top battery was genuine but the bottom one I had hollowed out and used as a hiding place for important messages. A couple of days before I had received from Jean Beauchamp the names and addresses of various individuals whom he proposed to recruit as operators and cut-outs. I had intended to memorise these and in the meanwhile had written them down in the first part of my cipher before it was "closed"—which was as easy for me to read as ordinary text—and if found would make my cipher easily "breakable" by any competent cryptographer. This would be a disaster which, among other things, would lead to the arrest of several more members of the network; and it would certainly be my death warrant if I ever fell into Russian hands.

To my horror my guard picked up the torch and began flicking the switch. Fortunately, when he found it did not work he merely laid it down again on the table. The torch was taken to prison along with all my other property and later I was able to apply for it, extract the messages, eat them (thereby following the best traditions of espionage), and breathe freely once more.

The search did not take long. The police found no difficulty in locating the hiding place for my transmitter because, as it was in use at the time of the raid, the door of the hiding place was open. After I had been in the flat for some time I had constructed a hiding place in a cavity about a built-in cupboard in my sitting room. So well did the join blend into the surrounding wall that both Pasche and Knecht admitted that had it been closed they might well have found considerable difficulty in discovering it. At that time all it contained was my cash reserve. The police were, however, a little apprehensive about booby traps and brought me back into the room so that I myself could extract what was in it under their eyes. A sensible precaution and one which I recommend to anyone dealing with a suspected saboteur or his equipment.

About three in the morning I was taken by car to police headquarters in Lausanne, and my interrogation by Pasche and Knecht began and continued until the following evening. At the time of my arrest they had been most jovial and the whole affair had been conducted, after the first rather sensational entry, in an atmosphere of complete international amity. There was, however, a complete change in their attitude once the interrogation began; they became very severe and grave. Pasche opened the proceedings as he was really in charge of the case, Knecht being federal police chief for the canton of Geneva.

The former made me a long and impressive speech. "It is useless for you to deny your activities, Foote," he said. "The suspects Bolli and the two Hamels have all made long statements which incriminate you completely and all your activities are known. It is now only necessary for you to make a complete confession and you will be immediately released." He added that there was no suggestion that I had acted against Swiss interests and as far as he, personally, was concerned he inclined favourably towards me as I had been working against Germany—which was the only country in the world which threatened Swiss independence—even though I had been working for the Soviet Union and not for my own country.

I replied that I admitted nothing but if what he said was true I must obviously be a moderately important person in the service of a great power fighting for its life. I pointed out that in the eyes of the Soviet Union I had been arrested by a power which was an enemy—as any power not allied to Russia was so regarded by them. If I were released at once they would imagine that I had betrayed all their secrets in order to secure my release. Therefore I demanded that I remain locked up and, what was more, for a longer period than all the other arrested persons, as the charges against me appeared to be graver. I added that if the accusation that I had been working for a Soviet intelligence organisation was true, then the interrogation that I would get at a later stage from the Russians would be infinitely worse than anything the Swiss could do. All the Swiss police could do was imprison me; the Russians on the other hand could make me face a firing squad and I infinitely preferred a few years in a Swiss prison to a few minutes up against a Russian wall.

This line rather flummoxed Pasche; he was not used to suspects pleading to be locked up and refusing chances of liberty. He then almost begged me to make a statement and I replied that I might after I had had time to think it over and consult my lawyer. I was then told that according to the wartime emergency regulations under which I was held this was not allowed until the police had completed their case against me. They could thus hold me incommunicado indefinitely. After this the interrogation dragged on throughout the day and in the end degenerated into a general discussion when everything under the sun was discussed save the case in question. As evening fell, I was taken away from police headquarters and to the Bois Marmet prison where I was to spend the next ten months.

A few days later I was again visited by Pasche, Knecht, and other police officers, and told that in an hour's time I was to be cross-examined again and that this time I must tell everything I knew or it would be the worse for me. I suggested that the proceedings might be helped if a few bottles of scotch and schnapps were taken from my cellar, as they would help to pass the time away and also might loosen my tongue. I was taken out of my cell into the interrogation room and the typewriter was prepared with a nice new sheet of paper in it all ready to take down my confession. The paper was as virgin at the end of the interrogation as it had been at the start. With the aid of the scotch and the schnapps a good time was had by all, and if it did not advance the investigation much it at least cemented Anglo-Swiss relations. I can only hope that the next time I am arrested for espionage I will meet such kind and courteous interrogators.

Though they got nothing from me, I managed to learn a certain amount from them. They had no idea where Rado was hiding, but had got Cissie under surveillance and were letting her run loose in the hope that she would lead them to further contacts—particularly Lucy. They had of course found much of Lucy's material when they raided the Hamels' flat, and from the content of some of the messages, especially the one about the Oerlikon cannon, had deduced that Lucy was probably none other than their valued evaluator and source, Selzinger. This they confirmed, as the Lucy messages and the material he gave the Swiss General Staff were typed on the same machine. He was not arrested, however, till long after I was, and was then held in prison but three months before being released with a certificate from the General Staff.

I also learned that they knew of the plan of escape for the Hamels and Bolli, since they had deciphered some of the Centre's messages to Rado which mentioned it. As a result they had moved the three from Geneva, and they, too, were now in the Bois Marmet prison. They had been monitoring both Rado's and my transmissions for a long time and were now busy deciphering all Rado's back traffic to see if it would give them any new lines.

My time in prison was not unpleasant. For the first time in years I was able to relax completely, and I settled down to what I imagined would be a long stay as I did not believe it likely that I would

be released until the end of the war, by which time all my usefulness to the Centre would be over. Life in any prison is much the
same, and enough books have been written about it without my
adding to the number. I was allowed to wear my own clothes and
buy anything I wanted from outside, including one hot meal a day,
wine, tobacco, etc., so I did not do badly. I also had transferred to
the prison all my store of tinned food, of which I had accumulated
about enough to last me for a year if I had ever been forced to go
into hiding. Also, imagining that my stay was going to be a long
one, I gave up my flat, and the prison authorities obligingly stored
all my personal effects. I was thus able to settle down to a peaceful
period of eating and reading, and the days merged imperceptibly
one into the other. My cell was not uncomfortable though hardly
up to the standard of my flat. My principal complaint at first was
the noise of the other inmates pacing their cells. Bois Marmet
being a remand prison, most of the prisoners were awaiting trial
and not yet accustomed to prison life. Later I was transferred to a
"political" cell in the women's block which was a haven of peace
and quiet.

After the last schnapps party the Swiss police apparently gave
me up as a bad job, for I was not bothered again and was left in
peace to consume my stock of food and work my way gradually
through the prison library.

Early in September 1944, after I had been in prison for ten
months, I was visited by a certain Captain Blazer of the Swiss Army
Legal Branch. He stated that the federal police had completed their
case against me and the rest of the network (by this time they had
also arrested Cissie, Lucy, and Taylor) and had handed the case
over to the military for the latter to take any action they thought
fit. He added that there was no evidence that I had worked against
Swiss interests and that therefore I could be released on bail pend-
ing trial before a military tribunal if I would first of all sign a statement admitting that I had been working as a Soviet agent. This I
refused to do until I could consult my lawyer, whereupon Blazer
produced the article in the military code stating that persons de-
tained for espionage or offenses against the neutrality laws were

not entitled to legal aid until the case against them had been completed. The police had given me the same answer, though in this case I was given chapter and verse.

I had unfortunately to decline the offer, as it is one of the rules of the Centre that an arrested agent must never admit that he has been working for the Soviet Union. However, a day or so later Blazer came to visit me and said that he was desolated that a person who had worked against the only potential enemy of Switzerland, meaning of course Germany, should stay in prison. He suggested therefore that I sign a statement saying that I had been working for "one of the United Nations" and leave out all mention of the Soviet Union. This I agreed to, and after signing the statement and a check for two thousand francs for my bail I was released on September 8, 1944.

I went straight to a Lausanne hotel and sat down to think things out. Obviously it was impossible for me to do anything till I was certain that the Swiss police really had finished with me and that I was not under surveillance. After a week or so I was certain that at any rate for the moment I was not being shadowed and so started a tour of the various places of conspiracy in the hope of picking up contact again with Cissie, Pakbo, or Jean Beauchamp. I knew all their addresses of course, but for obvious reasons was not going to visit them there in case they were themselves being watched.

The first person I met was Jean. He told me that Rado had never been found by the police and that he and his wife had left Switzerland clandestinely for Paris only a few days before. Rado had told Jean that he would at once contact the Soviet military attaché in Paris and arrange for a courier to be sent to contact him (Jean) in order to re-establish communication and finance the network. Finances were in a very parlous state—far worse even than when I had been arrested. Among other debts, Rado owed the Swiss Communist Party some seventy-five thousand Swiss francs of which twelve thousand were owed to the Geneva branch. Most of this had been borrowed from third parties and they were pressing for repayment, which put the whole Party in a very difficult position.

I also picked up Pakbo at his place of conspiracy. He had never been arrested, though he said that the police were suspicious of him (presumably as a result of some clue left by Rado in his papers which the police seized at Hamel's flat). He believed that the reason he had not been pulled in for questioning was that the police had no concrete evidence. He had seen Rado only twice since the latter had gone into hiding the year before, but had maintained contact with him through Jean Beauchamp.

Pakbo said that his sources were still capable of producing information and he was anxious to get things going again. He was not in the least satisfied with Rado. The latter had gone off cheerfully saying that he would send a courier and money, but had quite omitted to settle any place of conspiracy or to arrange any passwords or recognition signs. In fact he felt that Rado's departure had been dictated more by panic rather than any desire to re-establish the network. Pakbo's personal position was not too easy. He had incurred heavy debts in keeping his sources alive during the time I was in prison and needed money urgently.

He told me one rather amusing incident which shows the ramifications that a spy network may produce. After my arrest Rado, still in hiding, wished to get a message to the Centre suggesting a possible new line of communication. He consulted Pakbo, who said that he might be able to get a message sent to Moscow through the medium of one of the Allies. Despite the reprimand Rado had received when he suggested taking refuge with the British, he thought this was an excellent plan. He therefore gave Pakbo a message in his cipher, asking if it could be sent on. Through one of his contacts, possibly Salter, Pakbo had the message given to the Chinese military attaché in Berne who re-enciphered it in his diplomatic code and despatched it to Chungking with a request that the Wai Chiao Pu (Ministry of Foreign Affairs) hand it on to the Russian Embassy for onward transmission to Moscow. I learnt when I was in Moscow that the message had arrived. The Centre were furious, for they knew that Rado's code was compromised by that time, and they made no reply. What the Chinese thought about the whole thing will unfortunately never be known.

Finally one night Cissie herself came to our place of conspiracy and all the threads were picked up again. She had been arrested in May of that year together with her daughter Tamara and a former German minister, Paul Boetcher, with whom she was living. At the same time they had arrested Lucy and the cut-out Taylor. Cissie told me that until her arrest she had not known that I had been arrested and had thought that I had merely broken contact with Rado when the latter was compromised and went into hiding, and she had hoped that one day I could contact her at our place of conspiracy. She had kept open her channels of communication with Lucy despite the arrests, and all her other sources were also ready and willing to begin functioning again as soon as there was a new resident director and a channel of communication—and of course the necessary funds. This lack of funds had made Cissie commit a cardinal mistake, one which Moscow was later to regard with the gravest suspicion.

Desperate for money after my disappearance and Rado's going underground, she had, against all the rules and regulations, telegraphed to a former cut-out of the organisation, one Hermina Rabinovitch, who was working for the I.L.O. in Canada. This message was sent through Isaac, who was one of Cissie's sources in Switzerland and whom she used as a safe deposit for compromising documents. In veiled language the message asked Hermina to go to the Soviet Legation in Ottawa and ask for ten thousand dollars to be sent to Cissie through the medium of a New York watch company whose Geneva agent would pay the money to Cissie. Knowing that the message would be given to the military attaché at the legation, she also gave news of Lucy and Rado and asked news of me. (This message is mentioned in the Royal Commission report on the Canadian spy case and the relevant extracts from the report showing the connection between our organisation and the Canadian network are given in Appendix C.)

This telegram was sent at a time when Cissie was under surveillance by the Swiss police, who also saw copies of all telegrams sent abroad. In Moscow it was believed that this was the first clue that the Allies got regarding the Canadian network and that it, together with other information in Swiss hands, had been handed over to the Allies by the Swiss, that through this the whole organisation was uncovered, and that the defection of Gouzenko had been but a minor contributory factor.

It was quite apparent to us both that before anything else was done it was essential to see Lucy. He had been released at the same time as I, and after a short delay we all three arranged to meet at the Restaurant Bolognesa in Kasernenstrasse in Zurich. Cissie and I arrived first and awaited with some curiosity the arrival of this agent who had his lines so deep into the innermost secrets of Hitler. A quiet, nondescript little man suddenly slipped into a chair at our table and sat down. It was Lucy himself. Anyone less like the spy of fiction it would be hard to imagine. Consequently he was exactly what was wanted for an agent in real life. Undistinguished-looking, of medium height, aged about fifty, with his mild eyes blinking behind glasses, he looked exactly like almost anyone to be found in any suburban train anywhere in the world.

It was not difficult for us to establish our identities. He had been shown photographs of Cissie and me when he had been in prison, and a few questions from us soon proved that he was Lucy. He said that despite the July purge he was still able to supply information from Werther, Olga, and his other sources as before, and indeed was most anxious for communication to be re-established so that he could send his material to the Centre regularly. During the ten months that I had been in prison Lucy had continued to supply information from his sources, but there had of course been no means of transmitting it to the Centre. Cissie had collected it and paid for it and it had all been deposited in Isaac's safe (he had diplomatic privileges so it was safe there). Lucy had, however, insisted that certain of his information be made available to the Allies—even if it could not go to the Centre direct. As a result Cissie had arranged, through a series of cut-outs, for certain selected items which affected the western front to be passed to the British. The items which had been so passed were marked with a red cross on the copies of the Lucy material kept in Isaac's safe so that if and when the information was sent to the Centre they could see exactly which items had been passed over to their allies.

It was obviously essential that someone should go to Paris as soon as possible in order to re-establish the network. Rado could and should have done so, but he had left without a word, having made no arrangements. The obvious person was I, as I had taken over the job of resident director after Rado went into hiding. Lucy therefore agreed to give me all the material he had, and I arranged with him and Cissie a system by which they could be contacted quickly and safely by any new resident director who might arrive. I also saw Pakbo a day or so later and made a similar arrangement with him and collected a large quantity of information which he had accumulated.

At this time, November 1944, France was in a state of chaos and all normal means of transportation had broken down. I therefore commissioned Jean Beauchamp to arrange my journey to Paris, telling him it must be as quickly as possible and without any nonsense about visas or passport formalities. Jean arranged matters with his usual efficiency. He gave me a rendezvous in a café near the Swiss frontier on the road to a French frontier town. He would be sitting at a table there with two people, one the chief of police and the other the president of the Committee of Liberation of the French town, and I was to hand them any money or documents that I had in case I was searched by the Swiss customs. After leaving Switzerland I would be joined in no-man's land by these two, who would pass me through the French control. The whole thing worked like a charm. I left Switzerland on my valid British passport and I was then joined by my two new friends and additional reinforcements in the shape of two young members of the Maquis with tommy guns who waved the French *douaniers* and frontier guards aside. Thus I entered France for the first time since the war started.

My documents were returned to me and I was given a safe-conduct for Paris and a seat was found for me in a car which was just about to leave for the capital. The journey was completely uneventful and late that night I arrived in Paris and took a bed off one of my fellow travellers.

The next morning I set off on my search for a Soviet official to whom I could tell my story.

16

The Edge of the Iron Curtain

My first port of call was, of course, the Soviet Embassy in the Rue de Grenelle. I approached it somewhat circumspectly as I did not know conditions in Paris, whether it was likely to be watched or whether the arrival of a stray person there would be conspicuous. I need not have worried: the place was in complete chaos. I was quite unable to discover anyone who knew anything, who or where anyone was, or what anyone was supposed to be doing; and it was only with the greatest difficulty that I found anyone who could understand any known Western language. The entire ground floor of the embassy was occupied by a seething mob of Russian ex-prisoners of war whose main object in life appeared to be attempting to cadge cigarettes off me. At last I managed to make linguistic contact with one of the less ferocious-looking types in the place who realised that I wanted to see some high official and he gave me an address in the Rue de Prony where he alleged there were some Russian officials who might be the ones I wanted. It was obviously useless to stay where I was, and anyway my stock of cigarettes was running low, so I went off to the address. There I found that the Soviet Military Mission had just arrived in the building (the former Lithuanian Legation) and was busy installing itself.

The doorkeeper below luckily spoke French, as he had been fighting in the Maquis for part of the war, and I told him that I wanted to see "the chief" as I had important news from Switzerland. After only a short delay I was ushered in to see Lieutenant Colonel Novikov, who appeared to be in charge at that time.

Novikov was a tall fair flying officer with more than the usual share of Slav charm. Unfortunately for me, this was his first visit outside Russia and he did not appear to have much knowledge of intelligence work. Things were not made easier by the fact that he was at this interview willing to talk only Russian and the conversation had to take place through his adjutant, who acted as interpreter. At first he was reluctant to accept me at my face value and to take any action regarding my request that he get in touch with the Centre about me. He told me later that before leaving Moscow he had been warned to be on his guard against *agents provocateurs* and had been instructed to treat all unknown visitors as such until the contrary could be proved. Fortunately, during this first interview, when conversation was at its stickiest, the Soviet naval attaché from London came into the room and took a hand. He was evidently an old hand at the game, and after a few questions he seemed convinced that I was genuine and advised Novikov to treat me as such. I feel sure that he himself had worked at some time for the Centre, as both Rado's and my cover names seemed familiar to him, and when he asked the cover names of our main sources the answers seemed to give him satisfaction—as if they tallied with his recollection.

Once confidence had been established, my first request to Novikov was to be put in touch with Rado since, as he had left Switzerland for Paris some weeks before, I felt quite sure he had arrived and made his number by that time. Novikov assured me, however, that he had not yet shown up. He then agreed to send off a cable to Moscow about me, giving my cover names and also the cover names of other members of the organisation such as Albert (Rado), Cissie, Pakbo, Lucy, etc., and ask for the control questions so that they could be put to me. He also agreed to send off the voluminous information that I had brought with me from Pakbo and Lucy.

This information was in French and German and Novikov explained that his cipher was designed only for messages in Russian. He therefore asked me to stay on legation premises and help with the translation. This took a day and a night, with me translating the material into English and Novikov's adjutant retranslating it into Russian. As a result, I had not finished this task till the morning of November 11, and I was then told that a reply to their telegram about me to the Centre could not be expected for about six days. They kindly offered me the hospitality of the legation in the meanwhile, but I refused as this would have meant being cooped up in a room all the time till the answer was received. I preferred to go to a hotel outside and take a chance that the fact that my papers were not in order would not be spotted. I therefore arranged a rendezvous with Novikov's adjutant for a week ahead, under cover of darkness, at the corner of the Rue de Prony.

I had some difficulty in finding a hotel, as all the big ones had been taken over by the Allies and most of the small ones were unwilling to let rooms for a period as they could make more money letting their rooms by the hour to soldiers and their companions, the usual establishments having all been closed by the police after the liberation on the grounds of collaboration. After a couple of failures I found a room with the aid of a couple of packets of cigarettes as a *douceur*. Accommodation was always a difficulty since, having neither an entry visa for France nor a *permis de séjour* for Paris, my papers, to say the least, were not in order and I would be liable to arrest if I were picked up in a police raid or reported by a zealous hotel manager. As a result I moved my hotel every few days until in the end I found an obliging hotelier who, realising that I was phony, blandly increased his charges tenfold in recognition of the fact that I remained there unmolested till I left the city.

I had chosen the right day to see Paris, as Churchill and Eden were with General de Gaulle at the Armistice Day celebrations. The enthusiasm of the French on seeing Churchill was tremendous and it was a memorable occasion for me also, since it was the first time I had seen the great war leader who, when I left England, was still in political outer darkness.

The adjutant kept the rendezvous a week later and told me that Novikov had received a reply from the Centre but that I was to come again the next evening as all the telegrams for me from the

Centre had not yet been deciphered. Accordingly I presented myself at the rendezvous again the next night and after the control
questions had been put and correctly answered the atmosphere
mellowed considerably and we all settled down to an enormous
dinner liberally washed down with vodka and wine.

The Centre had sent a whole series of questions for me to answer, most of them pertinent and most of them not unnaturally
concerning the fate of the organisation. One or two, however, were
rather odd; for example: "Were agents of the Abwehr present when
you were interrogated by the Swiss police?" I assume that they
thought my arrest had been entirely the result of Abwehr tip-offs
and that there was a much closer liaison between the Bupo and
the Abwehr than in fact was the case; unless, of course, it was a
trick question of such subtlety that I failed to see the point. The
director was also very much concerned over the fate of Rado and
asked Novikov to find out discreetly whether he had not perhaps
been arrested by the French police.

In my first message to the Centre I had pointed out that the
network in Switzerland was completely intact and that all it needed
was a means of communication and funds; it could then continue
exactly as before. I had suggested that a new transmitter be installed either in Geneva or just over the frontier in French Com-
munist-controlled Annemasse, with the local French and Swiss
Communist parties running a system of couriers from the main
cut-outs in Switzerland. The director preferred the second plan and
I was instructed to work out a detailed organisation for this.

After the banquet was over and the messages had been discussed, I was told to make regular calls on the Military Mission
every two or three days under cover of darkness. The Mission in
the meanwhile had moved to the former Esthonian Legation in the
Rue du Général Appert, where they had installed a short-wave
transmitter which speeded communications somewhat. At one of
the visits I was ordered to go ahead with the plan for setting up
the headquarters of the Swiss network in Annemasse and also informed that shortly a false Dutch passport and a new cipher would
be sent me by courier.

Soon afterwards I was told that all plans had changed and that I was first of all to go to Moscow for discussions. I would be flown there on the return journey of the plane which was to bring Maurice Thorez back to France. The plane arrived towards the end of November and was due to return after a couple of days. It did not do so, however, as the pilot and the crew were busy sampling the delights of life outside the Iron Curtain and had not the slightest desire to leave the fleshpots of the decadent democracies for the husks of pure Marxism in Moscow. As a result all sorts of ingenious excuses were thought up by the crew for delaying the return trip, ranging from mechanical defects and bad flying weather through veiled suggestions of sabotage by the wicked Allies to plain illness of one of the crew. This pleasant game was put to an end by a stern signal from Moscow ordering them to leave the next day or be shot when they did return; but they had had their fun.

In the meanwhile an interesting situation had developed in the Rue du Général Appert. One evening, on one of my routine calls to the Mission, I was amazed to see Rado sitting in the waiting room. My surprise was nothing to Rado's. I knew that he had left Switzerland en route for Paris. He, on the other hand, had thought I was still incarcerated in a Swiss prison. Despite this, our training held and, as good secret agents, we neither of us showed any signs of recognition there. Only later when we were both summoned into the presence of Novikov did we speak to each other. Novikov said that no good purpose would be served by discussing then and there the whys and wherefores of the breakup of the Swiss organisation. He added that we were both going to Moscow, where the matter could be thrashed out in detail and at leisure, and that we were both to travel by the same plane. He also suggested that as there would be other passengers it would be better, from a security point of view, if we travelled as strangers.

This rather difficult interview was followed by the usual banquet. At it, for the first time, I saw Rado affected by alcohol. He confessed later that it was the first time for many years that he had drunk more than one glass of spirits at one time. If one got out of a Russian dinner having consumed ten times that quantity,

one was doing very well. During the course of this convivial dinner—convivial on the surface but with certain rather sinister undercurrents—every subject was discussed save the Swiss network.
Despite Rado's libations he acted rather as the skeleton at the feast.
The only fact of interest that I learned was that he had arrived about
a fortnight before.

This gave me furiously to think. For a fortnight I had been kept
ignorant of the fact that Rado had arrived, despite the fact that he
had seen Novikov and that Novikov knew that I wanted to see Rado.
We had obviously been deliberately kept apart until both our stories had been taken and there was no longer any risk of our com-
paring notes and concocting a coordinated story. Rado's arrival
had also coincided with the "change of plan" by which I was no
longer to go to Annemasse as a Dutchman but to return to Moscow
for "consultations." Obviously Moscow was not satisfied with the
Swiss setup and it seemed equally likely that Rado had put in a
story which differed radically from mine. Rado was, of course,
unaware that I had overstepped all the normal espionage rules and
had, in fact, contacted all our sources after my release from prison.
He assumed, therefore, that I was ignorant of the state of the network after Rado had left it in the air and thought that I was in no
position to contradict him.

Moscow, therefore, was determined to have us both back there
together so that they could cross-examine us at leisure and compare one story against the other. This did not particularly bother
me. Admittedly, Rado was a theoretical colonel and a man of high
standing with the Centre, while I was only an equally bogus major,
unknown personally to anyone at the Centre and of comparatively
new standing. On the other hand, the account I had given to the
Centre via Novikov was true in every respect and could easily be
checked by reference back to Switzerland. Similarly, all my accounts were in order and could be checked by anyone and found to
be correct to a dollar. Also in my favour was the fact that I had left
Switzerland having made all arrangements by which a new resident director could pick up the threads easily and quickly; while
Rado on the other hand had escaped in a hurry, leaving everything

completely in the air and having made no arrangements for any continuity. In theory and in fact my position was impeccable—if only Moscow would realise it and take the trouble to check the work of an unknown agent against that of an agent who had worked for the Centre for years. I looked forward to the trip to Moscow with somewhat mixed feelings.

For some time I had been considering my position vis-à-vis the Russians. Indeed, for a long time I had been disillusioned and unhappy about the attitude of the Centre. It was entirely ruthless, with no sense of honour, obligation, or decency towards its servants. They were used as long as they were of any value and then cast aside with no compunction and no compensation. The director expected miracles from the agents and the local Communist parties, and when the miracles were performed, there were no thanks and only a formal acknowledgment. Similarly, when the Centre demanded the impossible or the foolish—or both—and it was pointed out to them that the action would either end in disaster or frustration, there was never any sign that they had learnt a lesson or that they had any symptoms of contrition. Some of these attributes are no doubt common to all intelligence services, but the cold-bloodedness of the Centre and its lack of any common humanity or decency made it stand alone.

I argued to myself that I could not consciously and deliberately desert the work and throw my hand in altogether. It would have been perfectly easy for me to go to the British diplomatic or service authorities in Paris and explain who and what I was and get speedy repatriation to England. Similarly, I could throw a brick through a Paris police station window and get myself arrested, with an exactly similar result. But this I would not do. The war was still on and the information available in Switzerland was useful, if not vital, to the Russians—who were Allies. It was clearly my duty to do all I could to get the network against Germany working again. Deliberately to desert the work would have been in my eyes equivalent to desertion in the face of the enemy. On the other hand, I argued that if once I got to Moscow it might be many years before I saw Europe again, if at all, and all my desires to get the Swiss network re-established so as to extract the vital information out of Germany might be equally frustrated by suspicious Kremlin officials.

In the end I made no decision one way or the other and left the whole thing in the lap of the gods. I made no attempt to get myself arrested or to contact the British or Americans. On the other hand, I continued to live in hotels and to move freely round the town as if I had been the best-, rather than the worst-, documented Englishman in Paris. At the time the police were making frequent raids and setting up unexpected check points in the city in an endeavour to catch deserters and also to check up on the many alleged Abwehr agents who were supposed to have been left behind at the time of the liberation. In addition, there were, of course, the various swoops and checkups by the military police of the Allies.

Soon after I had come to my decision I thought that the matter was quite definitely going to be taken out of my hands. I was on my way to my favourite restaurant, Chez Mermoz, in the Rue de Tremoille, for dinner and had taken the Métro and got out at Marbœuf only to find that the police had blocked all the exits and were examining all papers. I was last in the queue and felt a certain relief that finally the future had been taken out of my hands and that I need think and plan no more. I presented my visaless and unstamped passport for inspection. The inspector in charge of the point saluted and waved me on without a glance. The dice appeared definitely cast for Moscow.

Despite my rather troubled mind I enjoyed my stay in Paris. It was pleasant to be able to pass the time without any thought of immediate work, and a good meal often did much to dispel the nagging doubts about what I should do and how I should do it. I courted all kinds of dangers which lurked for anyone in my visaless state. Never once, the whole time I was in Paris, was I asked for my papers though my stamping grounds ranged from the blackest of black market restaurants to American officers' messes.

All things come to an end in time and on January 6, 1945, at nine in the morning, I took off for Moscow in the first Soviet plane to leave France since the liberation. The plane was alleged to be carrying Russian prisoners of war being repatriated to Russia, but this was a convenient Soviet fiction. How hollow a fiction it was can be seen from the fact that the plane had four vacant seats despite the equally hard fact that there were over a million Russian prisoners of war in France clamouring for repatriation. It is perhaps pertinent also to note that in our planeload there was in fact only one genuine Russian prisoner of war.

All the passengers held Russian repatriation certificates. Certificate No. 1 was held by a veteran Bolshevik, Myasnikoff. A likable old ruffian, looking like a venerable edition of Maxim Gorki, he had led the general strike in Russia in the early 1920s which almost overthrew Lenin and Trotsky. Trotsky had wanted him shot but Lenin had overruled this and he had merely been exiled to Siberia. He was offered a pardon if he cared to return to European Russia, which he had accepted. Later he had again been exiled. This time he had escaped to Turkey and from there had come to France, where Briand offered him asylum. During the war years he had been in hiding, as the Germans were after him, and after the liberation he had been seen by Bogomolov, who had offered him a pardon and an important post in Moscow if he would return. Thorez had offered him the same, and Myasnikoff showed me a letter signed by Thorez when the latter had been in Moscow, couched in similar terms. He had no liking for Stalin and I think had little real hope that the promises would be honoured. I never saw or heard of him again after I reached Moscow, nor have I ever seen his name in the press. It is more than likely that he is now tasting Siberian exile for the third time. He had an extremely alert brain and did much to lighten the tedium of the journey.

Certificate No. 3 was held by Alexander Koulicheff, who was Rado. Certificate No. 4 was used by a certain Ivanovsky, also a Soviet agent of questionable nationality. He spoke Russian and French fluently and some English. I gather that he had spent some if not most of the war in hiding in France. I know nothing more about him but that he was a most charming travelling companion. The holder of certificate No. 5 was the only genuine prisoner of war on the plane. His patronymic I have forgotten but he was known to all of us as Vladimir. A virile young tough, he had been a submarine commander in the Red Navy before he had been captured, and he had been decorated as a "Hero of the Soviet Union." On his escape he had organised the Vladimir Group of the French Resistance and had twice been decorated by the French for his activities as a partisan. There were also on board a diplomat from London, Smirnov, and another diplomat and his wife.

Certificate No. 2 was held by Alfred Fedorovitch Lapidus, former Esthonian national, now a Soviet citizen, who had been deported from Tallinn to France by the Germans. In fact, none other than myself.

This was the planeload of "returning P.O.W.s," and a nice representative collection it was, too. As regards the real P.O.W.s, no such luxury as a plane ride back to the Soviet Union was in store for them. They were first checked to determine their degree of collaboration with the enemy and then again checked to find out why they had disobeyed Stalin's order to fight to the death. Very few of them on their return found that liberty in their homeland for which they had fought. The majority of them were drafted into labour camps, where they will remain till they die or are worked to death— not that there is much difference between the two. The Soviet state has very short shrift for those who do not obey implicitly, and the labour camps are always hungry for new blood.

The journey to Cairo was as uneventful and boring as all air travel. I had not flown for many years and at first it was interesting to look down at the French landscape and to observe the precision with which the Allied air forces had bombed the bridges and the airfields over which we flew. After Marseilles, where we stopped the night, there was only the Mediterranean and then the endless tedium of the North African coast. It was dark by the time we reached the Egyptian border and so the battlefield of El Alamein was hidden from us. The only breaks in the tedium were the two nights we spent at Marseilles and Castel Benito, where we were guests of the R.A.F. in their mess. As the first Soviet planeload through, we were objects of some curiosity and equally targets for the traditional R.A.F. hospitality. Liberally entertained in the mess, we were sent off each morning laden with chocolate, tobacco, and whiskey. I spent a large portion of the night at Castel Benito telling a large crowd of officers about my experiences as a prisoner of the Nazis. It was with some difficulty that I kept my face straight and my character up as Lapidus, the exiled Esthonian, in a mixture of bad English and French.

We were due to spend two nights in Cairo and as a result did not stay at the airport, but went into town and were billeted at the Luna Park. Accommodation, as always in Cairo during the war, was short and the manager said that we would have to share rooms. Rather to my surprise Rado spoke up; it was almost the first time he had opened his mouth since we had left Le Bourget, and said that he would share with me if I was agreeable.

I cannot say that he was a lively room companion. The first night he hardly said a word and declined to come out with me into Cairo for a final fling. On my return from a pleasant and convivial evening he was asleep—or pretending to be. The second evening he was, if possible, even more depressed but did become somewhat loquacious. He said that he feared we were in for a difficult time in Moscow, and compared our situation to that of a captain who has lost his ship. No explanation would convince the director that it had not been our fault that we had lost the sources which the Centre valued so highly.

I attempted to reason with him and calm his fears. I pointed out that my arrest and the consequent breakdown of communications had been entirely the fault of the Centre. They had ordered transmissions to continue after the arrest of the Hamels and Bolli, when they knew that the heat was on. Also they had never given us sufficient funds to provide an adequate reserve of trained operators and spare transmitters. In any case, I added, the main sources, Werther and Olga and the others, still remained and could be made instantly available as soon as communications were re-established. Also the Centre had not been deprived of these sources altogether, as I had brought a quantity of material with me to Paris which had been sent back to Moscow; so that they had in fact the cream of all the material available for the year November 1943–November 1944 when the Swiss network had been out of touch.

This information really startled Rado and he became more depressed than before. He bewailed the fact that he had not discussed the matter with me in Paris. Rather unkindly, I pointed out that he had only himself to blame, as I had given him my address after our first meeting at the dinner and he had not bothered to come round. It was entirely his own fault that he was going to Moscow unaware of the true state of affairs, and as an old hand at the game, he must know the danger of putting in reports without bothering to see if they tallied with the facts.

There was a long silence after this, while Rado sat tapping his fingers on the small hotel table, lost in thought. Then he got up and left the room without a word. I never saw him again. The plane left next morning without him, and his hat, coat, and luggage remained in the hotel bedroom uncollected, mute evidence of a spy who had lost his nerve.

At six the next morning we took off again, and when we reached Teheran we were delayed for three days by bad weather. I spent most of the time with Myasnikoff, who was a much more entertaining roommate than poor Rado. He expressed his relief at having got out of the sphere of British influence with no difficulty. He confessed that he had been nervous, as he had ordered the shooting of a number of British officers as a reprisal for the execution of the commissars in Baku during the period of foreign intervention. He also said that he thought his past might be brought up against him as he, as high commissioner for the Urals, had ordered the execution of the Czar and the imperial family at Ekaterinburg against the strict orders of Lenin. He made no secret of his dislike for Stalin, whom he had known in Baku in the pre-Revolutionary days. At that time he was a brighter light in the Party than Stalin and on two occasions had had Stalin expelled from the Party for brigandage. This was a curious echo from that part of Stalin's less respectable past when, no doubt for the highest political motives, he had been engaged in several bank robberies in Georgia with his own small coterie who believed that brigandage was the best way to world revolution.

After a night in Baku, where we were met by the N.K.V.D., who got us through the customs and passport formalities with speed and ease, we took off for Moscow. We were to have been met in Baku by officials from the Centre, but they missed us, as we had changed planes at Teheran and they were waiting for the wrong plane.

When we had left Baku Myasnikoff got the pilot to send a signal to the airport to ask Molotov to send a car to meet him. (He was in fact met by one of the state Packards, but the grim faces of the escort made me think it unlikely that a very rosy future lay ahead for this man, one of the last veterans of the Revolution.)

At four o'clock on the afternoon of January 14, 1945, the plane touched down at the airport in Moscow. I was well and truly behind the Iron Curtain.

17

THE IRON CURTAIN CLOSES

We had not landed at the main Moscow airport, but at one of the smaller ones on the outskirts of the city. In fact only as we were coming down was it possible to catch a glimpse of the capital. It appeared quite unbombed and indeed untouched by war. Like most buildings in Moscow, the airport had a shabby air and the concrete waiting hall was unadorned by any decoration nor was it warmed by any central heating, which would have been welcome as it was bitterly cold with snow on the ground. The only gesture towards luxury was a small wooden booth selling fruit juice.

I was met by two characters, a man and a woman. The man was a nondescript individual whom I was never to see again. The woman, whom I knew as "Vera," was dressed as a major in the Red Army. Aged about forty, with raven hair, she must have been quite a beauty in her youth. She spoke fluent English, French, and German, so there was no language difficulty at all.

With her and her companion, or possibly it might he more suitable to call him chaperone, as his duties were purely those of an escort, we drove to 29 the 2nd Izvoznia Ulitza, which was to be my home for the next eighteen months. This was a comparatively modern block of flats and, apart from myself, was occupied by the wives of generals who were away fighting at the front. In my flat, which consisted of a bedroom and a sitting room, I was introduced to Olga Pugachova, my housekeeper, her eight-year-old daughter, Ludmilla, and Ivan, my permanent interpreter who I was told would live with me. Interpreter, escort, guard, all in one. Olga was a pleasant woman, the widow of a lieutenant colonel in the Red Air Force. For a variety of reasons which will be explained later, I think she enjoyed her time as housekeeper. After the introductions we settled down to the usual banquet, which was ready and waiting for us in the flat.

At the banquet, attended by Vera and Ivan, no business was discussed, but when Vera left she said she would come again in the morning with a number of questions to which she would like the answers. She was as good as her word and turned up again the next morning with a list of questions as long as my arm. She was also considerate enough to bring along a nice new German typewriter on which I could write my answers. Before settling down to the questions we had a long discussion on the whole situation in general and Rado's mysterious disappearance in particular. Vera was perfectly *au fait* with the whole organisation of the network— and indeed knew more about the identities of some of the agents than I did. This was not surprising, since before she had been posted to the Centre she had been in Switzerland and in fact had been the resident director there before Rado. As a result she knew all of the prewar sources not only by name but from personal experience. In addition to this, she was the officer who had run the Swiss network all through the war from Moscow and knew all our difficulties and all the various transactions, trials, and tribulations in which we had been entangled.

Vera finally left me with the list of questions, and after studying them I was, to say the least, far from happy. It was obvious from the tone of the questions that the Centre regarded me as an *agent provocateur* planted on them by the British. It was equally apparent that Rado's report (which had been telegraphed to the Centre about a fortnight after mine) gave quite a different version of the story. He had obviously stated that all our Swiss sources were either liquidated or compromised and that at least a couple of years should be allowed to elapse before any effort was made to revive either them or the network.

In the view of the director I had obviously been released by the Swiss police on British intervention, the British *quid pro quo* being that I would transmit to the Centre only such information as the British would supply, though attributing it to the various sources known to Moscow. The British object in all this being, of course, to hinder the advance of the Red Army by feeding them false information. Equally the director was certain that Rado had been conveniently "liquidated" in Cairo by the British to prevent his giving a different story to Moscow. I was by now comparatively inured to the Soviet conception of Allied cooperation, after my experience with Rado at the time he wished to go into hiding, but this fairly took my breath away. Fantastic as the whole thing was, the Centre obviously believed quite seriously that the British would, in the middle of a war when all the Allies were fighting for their lives, settle down to produce as complicated a plan as this, merely to deceive their allies. The whole conception could only have been bred in brains to whom treachery, double-crossing, and betrayal were second nature. It was, in the abstract, high farce; but, like so much farce, in the concrete it bordered on high tragedy as far as I was concerned. Unless I could clear myself I was obviously in for a very difficult period and might only too easily find myself against a wall as a British spy—which, regarded impersonally, was an interesting twist of fate, but which personally I regarded with the utmost disfavor. If, in addition to all this, Rado was tiresome enough to commit suicide and his body was fished out of the Nile or found in a Cairo back street, then the final factual coping stone would have been put to the elaborate structure of fancy erected by the Centre.

In the meanwhile there was obviously nothing for me to do save fill in the questionnaires and answer the questions fully and truthfully. Luckily my conscience was perfectly clear and I could and did answer all the long lists of queries accurately. The system was ingenious and, though it took time, was extremely effective. No pressure was ever brought to bear on me in any shape or form. With the utmost kindness and courtesy the various lists of questions were put to me over a period of weeks. Many of the questions overlapped and dovetailed into others which may have been asked days or weeks before. Questions, apparently put at random, were in fact cross-checks on other points that may have arisen only in casual conversation. As a result, at the end of the time my interrogators—if I can call them that, as I knew them only on paper—had not only the whole story but a complicated, overlapping, interlocking series of questions and answers. Luckily I was telling the truth and so the answers were consistent and easy to give. It would need a very clever man with a very elaborate and word-perfect cover story to stand up to such a test, for the slightest discrepancy would show up at once and give the unseen interrogators more ammunition to break the story down.

During this period of question and answer I was not kept a prisoner in any sort of way. Vera said that I was perfectly free to walk about the streets as much as I liked, provided of course that I was accompanied by Ivan. She did recommend that I stick to the side streets, because if I walked down the main streets I might be picked up for questioning by the police as a foreigner, which might be embarrassing. On several evenings I was taken to the theatre. Tickets were obtainable only on priority and thus not only the spectators but also the allocation of seats were government-controlled. It was not coincidence that on several occasions when I went to the theatre I found myself sitting between English or American officers. Nor was it coincidence that in the seats behind me were sitting a couple of hard-faced individuals who appeared more interested in the row in front than in the scene on the stage. I can also hardly believe that it was a demonstration of inter-Allied amity which made Ivan take me for a walk one day and show me the British Embassy. They were still obviously convinced that I was a British double agent and were giving me every opportunity to prove it and as much rope as I wanted in order to hang myself. It frequently occurred to me that if in fact I *had* been a British agent the last thing I would have done would have been to talk to anyone in a theatre or go to the British Embassy. The Centre might have credited me and British Intelligence with better sense than that.

The one bright spot to lighten these rather dark days was the news, about a month after I arrived, that the Egyptian police had located Rado and that the Centre were sending someone to interview him. I do not think I was told this news out of any consideration for me, but merely to see my reaction to it. Later I was told that he had been interviewed by an emissary from the Centre but had refused to continue his journey or to give any reasons for his refusal.

About a fortnight after that, roughly six weeks after my arrival, I was told by Vera that the next day the director himself and some others would be coming to see me. Punctual to the minute, at six the next evening the director arrived. He was accompanied by a couple of stern-looking gentry who were either minor members of the Centre or members of the N.K.V.D. In any case they played little part in the events of the evening, spending most of the time looking hard at my face to judge my reactions to the various questions shot at me. I was told that the director held the rank of lieutenant general. That he was high up in the hierarchy could be seen from his car. The easiest and by far the best touchstone as regards the importance of an individual in the Union is the size and grandeur of his automobile. If (as the director had) he has a large, new black limousine, then one can be sure he is pretty important. If in addition to that he has a bodyguard, then he is more important still. If he has not only a fine new limousine but also another car to house the bodyguard, then one is certain he is a very big shot indeed. The director fell into the last category, and I was suitably impressed.

Outwardly nothing could have been more convivial and pleasant than the early stages of that dinner. A casual eavesdropper would have been enchanted at the sight of so great a man graciously at his ease with an honoured guest. The undercurrents were not so pleasant. I was irresistibly and unpleasantly reminded of a story told me by a former czarist cavalry officer friend of mine in Switzerland. Before the first World War he had been stationed in Siberia, where the tedium got too much for them at times. To lighten the boredom of their existence they used occasionally to have a large and sumptuous banquet. At the end of it they would all draw their revolvers and throw them in the middle of the table, where they would be shuffled by the orderlies. One pistol would be loaded. At a given signal they would all put a gun to their heads and pull the trigger. My friend said that the thought that at the end of the meal one of his comrades, or himself, would be a corpse added spice to the feast. I felt rather the same, only in this case I knew only too well who the corpse would be.

The director was a charming individual. Like so many of the high officials whom I saw, he did not seem a true Slav, but had more of a Georgian cast of countenance. In his early forties, he was intelligent and intellectual, and looked it. He spoke fluent, almost faultless English and had obviously spent some time in the United Kingdom; his occasional lapses into Americanese indicated that he may also have seen service in the States. I was to learn in the course of the evening that he spoke equally good French and German. The only point of criticism that I could find was his taste in ties, which was gaudy in the extreme. This may have been a relic of his American days. In addition to all this, he was a first-class interrogator. From my rather scanty knowledge of him, derived from the few meetings we had together, I should think that he was admirably fitted for his job. He had a heavy responsibility to bear as he was, I believe, directly responsible to Stalin himself, and according to Vera was one of the few people in the Soviet Union who could see Stalin without an appointment. He also had a direct private line to Stalin's office.

The interrogation lasted from six in the evening till two the next morning and continued over and after the food. The four of them, the director, Vera, and the other two, had what I assume was my dossier in front of them and occasionally they would produce from it a telegram that I had sent and question me as to its contents and how it had come to me. They went through my whole career with the Centre very closely and questioned me minutely on all the various sources that we had. They were especially interested in Lucy and Pakbo and wished to know who Lucy's sources were and how they reached the network so quickly. On this point I was of course as ignorant as they were.

The director stated that usually Lucy's information had been correct but once it had proved disastrous. He pulled a telegram out of the dossier and handed it to me. "Do you remember sending that?" he said. I looked at it; it gave details from Werther of troop dispositions on the eastern front. I replied that I had sent so many similar ones that I could not remember after the lapse of years anything about that particular one.

"That message cost us a hundred thousand men at Kharkov and resulted in the Germans reaching Stalingrad. It was sent over your transmitter," replied the director. "After we received this and saw the damage that it wrought we could only assume that Lucy was a double agent and all his information was false and supplied by the Abwehr. For a long time after that we ignored the information, convinced that it was planted on us. Only after months of checking did we decide that, as all the other information from that source was correct and could be proved correct, the source was after all reliable. The information must have been falsified after it left Germany. Perhaps, my dear Jim, you can throw some light on this?"

I could only reply that I received the Lucy information, already edited by Rado, either direct or via one of Rado's couriers. In the latter case it was always in a sealed envelope. I was also able to assure the director that I had never left the material lying about, so there was no question of substitution.

After the ordeal, when I felt completely sucked dry of all information and also extremely tired, as I had been at it for eight hours with my senses alert the whole time, I was asked to withdraw to my bedroom as the others "had some matters which they wished to discuss." I felt rather like the prisoner when the jury have withdrawn. After an interval—it may have been half an hour, though it felt like an age—the director joined me. He appeared to be in an extremely good humour and slapped me jovially on the back. He stated that the Swiss affair was not yet cleared up and would not be until the end of the war when a military mission would be sent to investigate the whole thing on the ground in Switzerland and Germany. In the meanwhile, there was nothing with which I could be reproached and as far as the Swiss debacle was concerned I was entirely exonerated and he thanked me for my efforts in Switzerland and also for my plans and attempts to re-establish the network after my release from jail. As regarded Lucy and Pakbo, he felt that I had been perhaps a little naïve.

"These two individuals were not motivated by ideological reasons but were primarily concerned with gain. There is no doubt that after their release from prison"—Pakbo, of course, had never been arrested but that was a minor matter— "they had obviously been approached by the British Secret Service who had seduced them away by gold in order that in the future they could send false information in order to hinder the advance of the victorious Red Army."

He regarded the fact that I had not been questioned by the British after my release as proof positive that Lucy had been "got at" by the British. He was quite satisfied that I had had nothing to do with this British plot and added that it was quite clever of the British not to approach me as it was not likely that I would put myself into the "Bear's embrace" if I had had a guilty conscience and had accepted a British offer to double-cross.

As regarded Rado, he said that measures were being taken to bring him to Moscow by force. Rado's refusal to come he attributed to pressure brought to bear by the British, who were threatening reprisals against Rado's wife, still in Paris. In any event he would come to Moscow in the end. "Very soon there will be no place in the world where it will be possible to hide from the Centre."

In the meanwhile he advised me to learn Russian as quickly as possible and said that a good job would be found for me in Moscow. It would be dangerous for me to go abroad for some time as my arrest would have "blown" me to all the counterespionage services in the world and no doubt the Swiss would have already supplied them with my particulars, fingerprints, etc. It would therefore be necessary to let things calm down for a period before I could be used abroad again.

When he left me I sank onto my bed exhausted. I was dog-tired physically and mentally. I slept like a log that night and woke late next morning. The sun was shining brightly and was reflected gaily off the glistening snow on the rooftops. Moscow was a pleasanter place than it had seemed for some weeks past. I might still be behind the Iron Curtain but my name was now cleared and, come what may, I was still free and alive—and that is a lot in Soviet Russia.

18

MOSCOW MISCELLANY

Many books have been written about life in Russia by outsiders in privileged positions and a few have been written by privileged Russians themselves. The number of the latter are so small that I have included here a chapter on life in Russia as it affected me—a privileged foreigner but living to all intents and purposes as a Russian. As a person with some training in observation and deduction it was interesting to see the Soviet way of life from the inside, and a brief note on what I found is perhaps worth recording.

Living problems in Russia divided themselves neatly up under three heads: food, housing, and heating, but all three were mutually interdependent since, if one category of food was obtained, then it was equally certain that a similar category of housing and heating would be available. Money did not really enter into it unless one was in the millionaire class, when all would have been available. Money was no criterion as regards the rations drawn and the privileges obtained; these depended entirely on position and work done. As far as that went, it could be said that the system was purely Communist and economically sound, as it based the standard of life of the individual on the service which he performed for the state. But into this neatly stacked deck of Communist cards there must be inserted the jokers of the black market and privilege by position, and these completely threw out of doctrinal gear the whole economic machine as applied to the individual.

Food was not rationed to the individual but was allocated by the state to the organisation or trades union to which the individual belonged and this organisation in its turn parcelled out the food on its quota to the particular individual—the amount depending upon the productive effort or the particular needs of the individual concerned. In practice this scheme applied only to rye bread and cabbage, the only foods the average worker obtained on his basic ration. Meat, butter, etc., were reserved for those in higher production groups or groups considered by the state more worthy of such luxuries.

These basic rations of bread and cabbage were issued only to workers and as a result everyone over the age of fourteen was bound to take a job in order to obtain what might seem to be the bare essentials of life. An exception was made for women with over two children under fourteen. They could obtain bread cards and certain other foods in the lower rationed category even though they did not work. If, however, they wished to obtain clothing coupons or supplementary rations over and above the basic, then they would have to go out and work. The other exceptions were the wives of generals and other Russians holding equivalent rank, who were excused from all work and received rations in a much higher category. If, in the case of generals' wives, their husbands were killed, these privileges continued; on the other hand, no widow of an ordinary Russian soldier killed in action received any sort of pension or privilege.

Generally speaking, there were three kinds of shops in Moscow. Those which sold goods against coupons and vouchers; those "commercial shops" which sold everything freely without coupons, vouchers, or any formality—but at a fantastic price; and the special shops where only privileged persons in certain categories could buy. In addition, there was the black market. Every effort by the Soviet authorities, ranging from executions and exile to education, had entirely failed to eradicate the "free market" and in 1945 it was flourishing as freely, and probably on the same sites, as it had in 1919 after the Revolution.

Before dealing with the more legal means of purchase, a word about the black market may not be amiss. The Moscow black markets often occupied the sites of the old peasant markets, or indeed any large open space, and in these were crammed as many as ten thousand buyers and sellers all taking the opportunity of buying goods at a price considerably less than that which prevailed in the "commercial shops." The militia made no attempt to control these activities but contented themselves with patrolling the approaches and seldom stopped anyone who was old, infirm, or crippled, as were the majority of the stall holders. On the other hand if any healthy or well-dressed individual was seen leaving the market he or she would almost certainly be taken to the nearest militia post and stripped. All cash and valuables and any commodities which might have been bought would then be removed from the arrested person and he would then be released, probably also without his shoes. As a result it was extremely rare for any respectable house-holder to deal in person with the black market. For example, my own housekeeper, Olga, was visited almost daily by an aged crone whose sole duty in life was to act as go-between for the more well-to-do housewives in their dealings with the black market. Though in theory illegal, the market received *de facto* if not *de jure* recognition from the authorities. On one occasion we failed to receive our weekly meat ration but instead we were sent some tins of canned fish and told that we could exchange this for meat on the black market!

Throughout my stay in Russia I dealt at the special shops. I gathered that there were hierarchies in these as in so many other things and that the best of all these shops were those reserved for the theatrical profession. In them a ballet dancer, film star, or junior lead, earning about the same salary as a factory hand, could buy goods at a tenth of the price that the latter would have to pay at a commercial shop. Furthermore many goods in short supply were to be found only in the special shops and never filtered down to the commercial ones—even at the fabulous prices which prevailed there. The second best special shops, I was told, were those reserved for the Foreign Office, where among other things, suits, shirts, etc., could be bought at prices and of a quality which would compare favorably with prices in the rest of the world. I was led to understand by my more cynically-minded friends that this was designed to lessen the shock to the budding Soviet diplomat abroad exposed to the first impact of Western standards.

The third class in these special shops were those designed for the General Staff and in these I was allowed to buy. There I could purchase on my official salary at least ten times the amount that any worker earning the same sum in roubles could buy himself—and I was being given a salary which was drawn by few workers—but even so no one could say that I lived luxuriously by any Western standard. In fact my salary seemed to vary around eighteen hundred to two thousand roubles a month. It never seemed to be fixed and some months I received more and occasionally I was told that I had been overpaid the month before. This gave me the equivalent of twelve hundred pounds a year but if I had drawn my salary in roubles and spent it on the open market I should have lived at just above starvation level. As it was I used to buy all my rations and necessities at the General Staff shop and these purchases were signed for and the amount automatically deducted from my salary. The remainder of my pay I drew in cash and little good it was to me save for occasional tips. The difference in price can be seen from the fact that a packet of twenty-five cigarettes in the commercial shops was 45/– while I purchased them for 4/6d. Similarly a box of matches which would be a penny farthing in the shop would be a few shillings in the open market.

I cannot complain as to my living conditions in Moscow. After all, I was living on the same scale as a Russian general. Equally there were no complaints from Olga or Ivan. Under Russian ration laws all the household draws the same ration as the head of the household and, as a result, while I was living in the flat they were drawing rations on the same scale as I. Nor when I first arrived in Russia were rations at all bad. The majority of the food that we drew was Lease-Lend material and we lived on excellent American canned products. After the end of the Japanese war, however, all Lease-Lend goods stopped and we then drew the equivalent amount of Russian rations and that was a very different thing. The food then, though still the same in quantity, deteriorated very quickly in quality; and the meat was often uneatable, and I for one got heartily sick of pickled cabbage—however excellent the quality.

As elsewhere in the world housing was a great problem in Moscow. A family which had more than one room could consider itself very lucky, or the head of the household was very privileged. Industrialisation has gone on apace but housing has lagged far behind. Factories and industrial undertakings were usually responsible for housing their employees but, faced with the difficulties of building and the shortage of supplies, they actually solved the housing problem by packing more people into the existing accommodation. Quite apart from the difficulties of building, the factories were also reluctant to build owing to the cost. Another factor that prevented building for workers was that all industrial undertakings were supposed to run at a profit and the heads of the organisations were reluctant to cut their paper profits and thus possibly incur wrath from higher up. This they would inevitably do if they indulged in building schemes, owing to the high cost of repairs and materials and the even higher cost of providing fuel for heating, which costs were inevitably far greater than any rent they might receive in return. Rent was limited to ten per cent of the tenant's income and in order to cover operating costs it was therefore necessary to pack every room to the absolute maximum.

The high building costs are also partially accounted for by the fact that it is only possible to carry out building operations during six months of the year owing to the climate. The building force, thrown out of work in the winter months, is usually occupied in snow-clearing, etc. The high operating costs are due to the high cost of fuel and the comparatively large labour force involved. Coal is in short supply in Russia and is not available for heating purposes save in public buildings. The usual winter fuel is wood and this has to be hauled, so far as Moscow and the large cities are concerned, from a long distance, as the forests near the large towns have been denuded long since. Wood-firing of the boilers means also that each block of flats must employ at least four and usually eight stokers and wood handlers as the boilers must be constantly fed throughout the twenty-four hours all winter long.

The block of flats in which I lived, 29 the 2nd Izvoznia Ulitza, was far from being a block of luxury flats by Western standards but would have seemed a paradise of luxury to the majority of the inhabitants of the Soviet Union. It had been built in 1938 as accommodation for the Red Army General Staff. It was also in sharp contrast to the surrounding jerry-built structures in having four-foot-thick walls and being built in an extremely solid fashion. This architectural style was not wholly in deference to the desire of the General Staff to be in a well-found building. The block was situated at a most convenient strategic position covering the important Mojaisk Chaussée and the Kiev Railway Station. I also noticed similarly well-constructed and solid fortresslike blocks of flats at other strategic points in the suburbs. It will be remembered that the planning of the Paris boulevards under the Second Empire was not only for aesthetic reasons but also to give the imperial artillery a clear field of fire. Similar allegations were made regarding the workers' flats built by the Socialists in Vienna. The Moscow town planners learnt a lesson from their predecessors in imperial France and Socialist Austria and neatly combined in one building comfort for their army staff and the means of gratifying the same staff's tactical requirements.

In this block I had, as already mentioned, a two-room flat. Olga slept in the dining room and in theory Ivan and I slept in the bedroom. In fact after the first night Ivan deserted me and for the rest of my stay preferred the company of the housekeeper; from the point of view of comfort if not of morals I did not regret the change. There was also a bathroom, but this was more in the nature of an ornament, as hot baths were forbidden by law, the hot-water system disconnected, and all warm water for washing had to be heated on a stove.

The black market, however, penetrated even into this block, and the stokers ran a black market shower bath in the basement. I went there only once. In semidarkness, with the floor covered with mud and slime, and with no privacy whatever, they had rigged up one jet in the ceiling under which, for the payment of an exorbitant sum, one could gyrate beneath a trickle of warm water. The smell and the state of the floor put me off after my one attempt but I used to see the generals' wives, often swathed in looted furs, waiting their turn with their husbands.

I tried the public baths but found the smell and the general dirt too much for me. Any such excursion also meant a four- or five-hour wait in a queue before obtaining the doubtful privilege of attempting to get oneself clean. A chit showing that you had had a bath within the past few days was also required before one could take a ticket on a second-class train. A sensible precaution, as the seats in these trains were soft and provided only too convenient resting places for the "minor horrors of war." However, these chits were also readily obtainable on the black market! In the end I gave up the struggle to wash myself like a Russian and contented my-self with washing in sections with the aid of a basin in the privacy of my own room. I at least knew then that any dirt I picked up was my own!

To run this block of fifty flats there was a staff of twenty-five: one "housemaster" and his secretary to control the staff and see that the tenants did not bring in unauthorised persons to share their flats; eight stokers and wood handlers; a plumber; an elec-trician; four lift attendants; four inside and two outside cleaners; and one guard in the courtyard to see that the washing was not stolen. At the end of the war when the generals returned home with their spoils of war, and after an armed robbery had occurred, two armed guards were added to patrol the place at night. (A general was entitled to one lorry load of loot and one private motorcar and with the return of the warriors our block became the wealthiest in the district.)

There have been complaints about the postwar crime wave in England but it is nothing to that which prevailed in Moscow when I was there. A large part of the city consisted of single-story log huts built long before the Revolution and conforming to no street plan. These rookeries had been long scheduled for demolition and as a result no repairs had been carried out and the place, with a multitude of boltholes in, out, and around the crazy structure, pro-vided an admirable hiding place for criminals. Indeed, effective control of the population there was so difficult and the number of gangsters harboured in them so great that during the time I was in Moscow these "Alsatias" were cordoned off by the militia between midnight and five in the morning. In addition there was a curfew from one to five and the streets were patrolled by cavalry who were inclined to shoot first and ask questions afterwards.

Crime was seldom if ever mentioned in the newspapers in Moscow, so that one knew only of those crimes which occurred in one's immediate neighbourhood. Never a week passed without one hearing of armed robbery, often accompanied by murder, in our district. The gangsters usually operated in large groups, one portion of the group committing the actual robbery and the rest manning the approaches to cover the getaway and often going so far as to put down holding fire to prevent the approach of any militia foolish enough to try to interfere. It was always impressed upon me that if ever I saw a robbery being committed—which, incidentally, would also include the clothes of the victim as well as the valuables—I was never to try to interfere as I was liable to be shot by the covering party.

During the war most of these gangsters were deserters (one division of Azerbaijan troops deserted during the winter of 1941-42 and terrorised the Moscow suburbs until the majority of them were rounded up). They were reinforced by deportees who had managed to escape from their guards on the way to labour camps and exile. I several times heard of whole trainloads of these overpowering their guards and then pillaging and ravaging the countryside. After the war the gangs received new blood in the form of demobilised soldiers who preferred a life of crime to the hunk of bread and handful of pickled cabbage which were the wages of industrial virtue. The most brutal of the gangs, which preferred on the whole to murder their victims as well as rob them, was the so-called "Polish Gang" which was alleged to consist of Polish deportees who had escaped and taken refuge in "Alsatia."

I am glad to say that I had no firsthand contact with these elements of disorder; my sole difficulty in Moscow arose out of a brush with the law.

On my arrival in Moscow the papers on which I had travelled were taken away and I had, for the first weeks, no sort of documentation at all. As a result Vera had warned me to take my walks in the back streets. After a bit, this prowling round the purlieus of Moscow did not suit me at all and, accompanied by the faithful—but protesting—Ivan, I went for a stroll down the Mojaisk Chaussée. Almost at once I was spotted by a plain-clothesman as a suspicious character or a foreigner (in Russia the terms are almost synonymous) and he tipped off the first militiaman on the beat to ask for our papers. The militia in Russia take the place of the uniformed police in the West and they deal with "petty crime" up to and including murder. Major crimes such as political heresy, Trotskyism, etc., are dealt with by the N.K.V.D., now the M.V.D.

Ivan had previously told me that if we were picked up I was to refuse to answer any questions and to demand to be taken to the nearest militia post, whence he would telephone to the Centre and obtain our release. Accordingly on the militiaman's demand Ivan refused to make any reply. This was not at all according to plan as far as the rather dense militiaman was concerned, and he at once assumed that he had at last got hold of a real enemy of the state. Whipping out his automatic, he invited us to put up our hands, which we declined to do; he then whistled up a colleague who telephoned to the militia post for a car. We were kept at pistol point in the street for a good half hour before a big black Zis drew up and out of it jumped the smallest but quite the most ferocious plain-clothesman I have ever seen. Before he was out of the car he started firing questions at us, his five feet nothing quivering with eagerness. The whole impression was slightly marred as he was also adorned with an extremely handsome black eye, no doubt a legacy of some previous heresy hunt. He bundled us all into the car and we were whisked off to the nearest militia H.Q. for questioning.

Ivan at once demanded to be allowed to telephone, but this the little man would not allow and said that if Ivan gave him the number he would ring up. This in turn Ivan could not do as the number of the Centre, even though it was changed every month, could not be divulged to third parties. Matters appeared to be at a deadlock and Ivan was then taken off into another room and stripped and searched. His papers, which of course they then found, described him as an officer of the General Staff and gave his previous job, which had in fact been on the General Staff but quite unconnected with the Centre's work. As a result when the N.K.V.D. rang up his unit all that they could say was that he had left his job a little time before on a special assignment about which they knew nothing.

They then turned their attention to me. Our original interrogator was now joined by a female N.K.V.D. lieutenant colonel who had quite the most evil face I have ever seen. She was a complete contrast to her colleague. He, like many small men, was explosive and excitable and danced round the room as he roared out his questions. She was cold and expressionless and regarded me as a snake does a rabbit, and indeed there was something very reptilian in her appearance and approach.

My knowledge of Russian was extremely slight at that time but I did manage to gather that they wanted my name and address. I contented myself with cursing them in all the languages I knew and using all the words in my not unextensive vocabulary. They did not appear impressed and I fear that it was wasted on them. In the end, enraged at the little man who thrust his face into mine, I cursed them both roundly in English, using the phrase usually rendered in polite society and print as "flick off." This had an immediate effect. My interrogators really thought that they were getting somewhere and at once wrote down on their paper "Name: Flick Off." I think they were somewhat impressed by the fact that I was well dressed and did not appear to be frightened of them, for they made no attempt to search me. After a further delay Ivan was allowed to dial the Centre's number himself and the N.KY.D. were told that we were to be released unquestioned. About a quarter of an hour later a car arrived from the Centre and we were driven home by a roundabout route so that the militia post would not know where we lived. This in fact was a useless precaution as we had been arrested quite close to the flat and in my future walks abroad I frequently met the original militiaman who had arrested me and also his colleagues from the same post, who had all got to know of

the mysterious foreigner who needed to have no papers. Whenever I saw them I was greeted with a broad grin and the salutation
of "Good day, Comrade Flick Off."

My first months in Moscow coincided with the ever-quicken-
ing collapse of Germany and the days were punctuated by the
booming of cannon and pyrotechnic displays to herald yet another
Soviet victory. These salutes were very effective at first but got tedious after a time and must have been an infernal nuisance to the
inhabitants of the jerry-built houses around ours, as there was a
battery in the neighbourhood which fired part of the victory sal-
vos and it must have shaken the flimsy houses considerably. In
general the Moscow public were singularly apathetic about the war
news. There were few newspapers in Moscow at that time save for
an occasional one stuck up on a bulletin board, and few people
appeared to look at the boards. All wireless receivers had been
confiscated earlier in the war but their place was taken by loudspeakers in the streets and squares which broadcast a continuous
programme of music and propaganda.

A quarter of an hour before the time for one of Stalin's Orders
of the Day proclaiming a victory a special announcer broke into
the programme and invited everyone to gather round and wait for
an important announcement which was shortly to be made. The
announcement was ultimately made, and very impressively it was
done, but few people stopped to listen to it. The only announcement they wanted was that saying the war was over at last. The
Russian propagandists had made the same mistake as Goebbels
with his *Sondermeldung* and all its impressive accompaniments
of Wagnerian music. Such things are all very well once or twice,
but frequent repetitions, however good the news may be, dull the
senses and breed contempt.

When VE Day did arrive the people of the Soviet Union remained in ignorance of it "for political reasons." Before it could be
announced Prague had to be liberated by Soviet troops and as a
result the Soviet Union had the dubious privilege of celebrating
their VE Day twenty-four hours after the rest of the world.

The director had sent me a short-wave receiving set soon after our last interview and as a result I was able to keep in touch with world news, even though electricity cuts (sometimes we got only one hour's electricity a day) prevented anything like continuous listening. I managed to pick up enough to show me that the war was over and by some mysterious means the whole population of Moscow also seemed to be aware of it—though there had been no official announcement.

The morning after all the other Allies had celebrated the end of the European war, Ivan told me that there was a rumour that Stalin himself would announce the defeat of Germany from the top of Lenin's tomb. Accordingly we both went to the Red Square where we joined the crowd of thousands who had heard the same rumour. There was an atmosphere of tense excitement which heightened and grew almost unbearable when the loudspeakers announced that an important announcement would shortly be made. There was a corresponding emotional slump when all that was announced was the Order of the Day on the capture of Prague and the list of generals who had taken part in the "historic battle."

As there was obviously nothing to be gained by looking at the Kremlin wall, the crowd moved off into the neighbouring Revolution Square where they cheered members of the staff of the American Embassy who appeared from time to time on the balcony. It was not till that evening that the long-awaited announcement was made over the wireless that the war was over and "the flag of freedom floated over Berlin." By that time most of the enthusiasm had evaporated and, though it was somewhat revived by the booming of the victory salutes and the firework displays, the crowd seemed content to wander aimlessly about the town looking in vain for someone to cheer.

The end of the war had its own particular importance to me as it had to everyone. To most it meant that there was a chance of going home and rejoining their families. To me it meant that my affairs would be cleared up speedily and I should probably be off on my work for the Centre again.

19
PREPARATION FOR A MISSION

In the last chapter I digressed from the main story to indulge in anecdotes about Moscow. The main thread was broken off at the meeting with the director.

Before he left me that memorable night when I felt I was on trial for my life, he had said that I would have to lie fallow in Russia for some time until things had quieted down and I had been forgotten by the counterespionage service of other powers. I protested violently against this. I explained with great force and eloquence that Russia had had its Revolution and that I had no intention of sitting quietly in Moscow when postwar conditions would make the rest of the world ripe for revolution. If the Centre was not prepared to use me for espionage work I demanded to be sent back to England to return to legal Party work there. This "revolutionary" zeal seemed to impress the director and he told me to work out a few alternative plans for possible espionage work abroad and put them down on paper for him to consider. We parted, with him convinced, I think, of my flaming enthusiasm for the cause in general and Soviet espionage in particular. That was the impression I wished to convey.

In fact my first six weeks in Moscow had convinced me that Nazi Germany as I had known it was a paradise of freedom as compared with Soviet Russia. I was determined to get out of it as soon as possible and return to a world where freedom was more than a propaganda phrase. The only way that I could get out alive was to feign enthusiasm for any espionage plan put up, carry on in Moscow as a good Communist till I was posted elsewhere, and then get out of the clutches of the Centre as fast as possible. I had done my best to help the Russians win their war but after I had seen them and their methods firsthand and at home I was determined not to help them win their peace.

I did not see the director again till about six months later, in September 1945, but I continued to receive lists of questions to answer; however, these now arrived only about once a week instead of almost daily. I duly replied to them and also sent off my suggestions regarding possible future employment. The only work I did for the Centre was to note down salient points of news and policy line which I was able to pick up from listening to foreign broadcasts on the short-wave set the director had sent me. About the time the set arrived I also received Soviet documentation which made me out to be Alexander Alexandrovitch Dymov, born in Madrid; the birthplace being of course to explain my faulty Russian.

Peace did not bring that return to normalcy which every Russian seemed to expect. The average inhabitant of Moscow seemed to have the idea that as soon as the shooting had stopped the shops would overnight fill with goods, the general theory being that these goods would be German. In fact the end of Lease-Lend resulted in a worsening of the ration for those who until then had been living on American goods bought in the special shops. Also, with the end of the war military movements seemed to go on at the same tempo. Many of the generals who came back from the West had only a few days' leave and then were transferred to the Southeast. The tension was not decreased by the construction and manning of even more balloon-barrage posts in and around Moscow after VE Day.

It was perfectly obvious from the talk of the generals, and especially their wives, and the propaganda line doled out by Vera, that the heat was about to be turned on Turkey and Iran. Vera explained the policy with great frankness. The war with Japan tied the hands of the Anglo-Saxon powers while neutral Russia had her

hands free and could achieve her ambitions in the Southeast without interference, for if the worst came to the worst she could always hold the threat of a deal with Japan over the heads of her late
allies. The dropping of the atom bomb put an end to this tense
situation and enabled Russia to get her cheap gains in the Far East,
though temporarily shelving her ambitions nearer home.

About six months after my arrival in Moscow, that is, about
July, I was told that Rado had been brought by force to Russia from
Cairo, and that I might be confronted with him. This never actually occurred but during the September visit from the director I
was told the end of the Swiss affair.

This call was far less formal than the last, as the director was
accompanied only by Vera and there were no skeletons in the shape
of N.K.V.D. officers at the usual feast which celebrated the visit.
The director stated that Rado had been intensively interrogated,
that a military mission had visited Switzerland, that the Centre
was investigating in Berlin, and that as a result of their findings
there was nothing with which I could be reproached.

Rado on the other hand would be shot for negligence in allowing his cipher to fall into the hands of the Swiss police, for falsely
reporting that the network in Switzerland was liquidated, and for
embezzling some fifty thousand dollars. The bait which had lured
Rado from the safety of Paris as far as the slums of Cairo had been
a promise by the Centre to pay him eighty thousand dollars to liquidate the alleged debts of the network in Switzerland and a promise that he would be allowed to return to Paris from Moscow after
a stay of only fourteen days. How an old fox like Rado fell for such
an obvious lure and embarked on the plane with me I cannot con-
ceive, as he must have known that his misdemeanours would ultimately be found out. His wife, Hélène, was still in Paris, but the
director said that steps were being taken to try to get her back to
Moscow. I do not know whether or not these were successful. She
was a woman of intelligence and I should think it unlikely that she
would put her head in the noose and go back to Moscow, in all
probability to join her husband against a wall or be sent to the
living death of an N.K.V.D. labour camp.

The director was also anxious to get Cissie back to Moscow and asked me if I could think up a suitable scheme to lure her there. She had apparently been interviewed by an agent of the Centre but had been reluctant to make the journey. In this she showed good sense, as the director had several bones to pick with her, not the least being her sending of the *en clair* telegram to Canada which the Centre was convinced had led to the unveiling of the Canadian spy case.

I was told that though it was against the general rule to send an agent abroad so soon after an assignment in which he had had trouble with the foreign police, the Centre were so short of good people that the director was making an exception in my case and was making arrangements for me to be sent off as soon as possible. He explained that the various networks in the United States had lain more or less fallow throughout the war but that they must now be rebuilt and reinforced as a matter of urgency in view of the "aggressive attitude" of that country. Before the war the network in the States had been principally occupied with industrial espionage, but now that the United States and Great Britain were the greatest potential enemies of the Soviet Union, all types of information were of great value and the network and sources were to be developed as fast and as extensively as possible.

As a result of wartime experience the main rules of the Centre, which had been occasionally allowed to lapse in the past, were to be rigidly enforced. All network chiefs were to live and direct their networks from outside the United States. I was to live in Mexico. There I would live on a genuine Canadian passport. The director added that they had not used the Canadian "cobbler" since before the war so that there might be some delay before the passport arrived. (See Appendix C.)

As a result of my new assignment I received from the Centre numerous books, magazines, newspapers, etc., published in Canada, America, and Mexico in order that I could "read myself in" and familiarise myself with recent developments in those countries. For practical as well as cover reasons the Centre always requires an agent to have a good working knowledge of the political trends in the countries in which he is living and against which he is working. As I had only one idea, namely to get out of Russia and quit the service of the Centre forever, I naturally feigned great enthusiasm for the project. At last freedom seemed almost possible.

Any idea of a speedy departure from Russia was knocked on the head in November when my health broke down and I became seriously ill with a duodenal ulcer. A legacy from the hectic days of my work for the network in Switzerland, it had not been improved by Russian food and got so bad that I was taken to hospital where I remained for a month and then had a further month in a convalescent home.

I was taken to the Central Military Hospital in Moscow, which was reserved for senior officers and their families, and there I was treated with great kindness and efficiency. The hospital was most competently run on lavish lines, with at least as many doctors and nurses as there were patients. The sanatorium at Bolshova whither I went after my time in hospital was equally comfortable and efficient and I have the happiest memories of this period of my life in Moscow.

I was something of a mystery to my fellow patients as I was an obvious foreigner though I had Soviet documentation. One theory was that I was a high-up German officer, and one elderly general at Bolshova tried to have a conversation with me about military tactics. It was there that I made probably my only contribution to culture and enlightenment during my stay in Russia.

Playing cards were illegal in Russia, but many of the officer patients had brought back packs with them from Germany. I therefore taught all the patients (the sanatorium was mixed, with a preponderance of women) all the gambling I knew. If anyone ever finds a Russian abroad with a profound knowledge of the complexities of gin rummy or stud poker he probably learnt it from me during those winter days in Bolshova.

I returned to the flat in the early days of 1946 but was soon informed that my assignment to Mexico was off as the Canadian spy case had made it impossible for them to get Canadian passports. Vera continued to visit me weekly and she was obviously deeply worried over the Canadian affair, as both she and the director were being blamed for having allowed the organisation to be run against all the rules and regulations.

I gathered that the resident director for Canada had been withdrawn sometime in 1941. Some time later the intelligence liaison member of the Canadian Communist Party had approached the official Soviet representative in Ottawa and informed him that they were in a position to obtain valuable scientific information. As, owing to wartime conditions, there was no possibility of sending out another resident director who could build up his network in the classic and secure way, the Centre was forced to organise on an *ad hoc* basis. They had been compelled to use regular members of the legation staff to handle the agents and sources, tasks for which they were not trained, and their position made them particularly vulnerable should anything go wrong. That something did go wrong, and disastrously so, is now history. The repercussions of the case spread far outside the bounds of Canada and affected the Centre's work all over the world, as, quite apart from internal organisational repercussions, it demonstrated clearly to the world Soviet postwar intelligence intentions.

The director and Vera were removed from their posts and replaced about May 1946. I never saw them again nor were they ever mentioned. The Centre has only one penalty for failure.

Vera was succeeded by one "Victor" who became my contact with the Centre. He had not Vera's long espionage background but he had had some prewar espionage experience in the United States. During the war he had had no connection with the Centre, having served as a staff officer. As a result of his prewar training he spoke excellent English and was in some ways a pleasanter character than Vera, who had been a little too much imbued with the atmosphere of the Centre to be an entirely agreeable companion.

A little later the new director came to visit me. Like his predecessor, he was not a pure Russian and was also possibly a Georgian, although he had a very Mongolian cast of features and an unimpressive personality, being short and rather squat. About his previous career I know nothing, and the only foreign language he appeared to speak with any fluency was German.

The director said that he was very anxious for me to go abroad on my new assignment as soon as possible. The one great delaying factor was documentation. He said that the Centre could produce admirable passports, as good as the originals if not better, but the day of the forged passport was over for the moment. Owing to post-war restrictions and controls, it was essential for an agent to have a passport whose number and particulars tallied exactly with the details in the central archives of the issuing country. In the old days when travel was easier and authorities less suspicious it had been enough to have a well-forged passport, such as the Special Department of the Centre could turn out in a matter of days. Nowa-days, however, there was a tendency for suspicious travel-control authorities to check up with central records and so only the genu-ine article would do.

There was no doubt from the director's and Victor's conversa-tion that the Centre's network in the States was in a bad way. Only a proportion of their agents had been uncovered or compromised by the Canadian affair, but the moral effect on the remainder had been great. The publicity accompanying the case had thoroughly put the wind up their various sources and many of them had "dried up" or firmly "gone private" rather than risk detection and the inevitable publicity which would have followed. The Centre was determined to build up the network again from the bottom.

The first result of the new director's decision to use me as soon as possible was my despatch in the early autumn of 1946 to one of the Centre's secret training establishments near the village of Sehjodnya, some twenty-five miles northwest of Moscow. The place had been used during the war to house a portion of the General Staff and then later had been turned into a prison for high-rank-ing German officers. There were many similar establishments in the neighbourhood, all under the control of the General Staff and some still used as prisons. In one, quite close by, was a group of czarist generals who had been taken prisoner while serving with the Japanese forces in Manchuria. These were shot about November. Other prisoners must have met a similar fate, as this was not the only time I heard the crackle of machine-gun fire at dawn.

The place, if somewhat primitive, was not uncomfortable. The main building was a sixteen-room log house standing in its own timbered grounds of about five acres. The whole was surrounded by a high wooden fence crowned with barbed wire. The staff, consisting of a housekeeper, a cook, and a maid of all work lived apart in a small log cabin in the grounds.

At this establishment I was to receive intensive training in the latest developments in the technicalities of espionage, ranging from microphotography to sabotage equipment and secret inks. This was the theory, but as so often in Russia the actual results in practice lagged far behind. I was the first pupil, and whether it was that the school was not yet properly organised or whether it was sheer incompetence I do not know, but in fact I learned singularly little during my time there. I lived in the house together with the director of the establishment, "Vladimir," a genial Georgian who spoke good German, having worked in Germany for the Centre before the war. In theory I was taught by instructors who came out to the house for the purpose. In fact I received instruction in radio procedure and technique from a teacher who knew little more than I did, and my instructor in photography appeared only twice, when he fell ill. I received some vague instructions in regard to secret ink, but the only details I can remember were on the use of pyramidon, which is developed by iodine, and this I had known of in Switzerland and knew it was a low-grade ink for secret use. In fairness to the Centre it is possible that they sent me there so that I should not think my time was being wasted, while they thought out ways and means of getting me abroad. I was later told, when I was on my way to Germany, that before I finally left on my mission I would be taken back to Moscow for a last-minute course in all the very latest developments.

At Sehjodnya I was visited frequently by Victor and on occasion by the director. Plan after plan, formulated to get me good documentation, was discussed and had finally to be discarded. In the end it was decided that I should be documented as a German and that my headquarters was to be the Argentine and not Mexico. My primary mission remained as always to set up an organisation to work in and against the United States. It was planned that I should arrive in Berlin ostensibly as a repatriated prisoner of war and take up a new identity and a new life there.

My life story as worked out by the Centre was as follows. I was a German, Albert Mueller, born in Riga in 1905, of a German father and an English mother. In 1919 my parents moved to Spain and there they both died, leaving me an orphan. I had later travelled to Cairo and the Far East and at the end of 1940 I had returned to Europe via the Trans-Siberian Railway to Koenigsberg in East Prussia in order to collect an inheritance which had been left me by my uncle. The authorities had not permitted me to return to the Far East and in 1942 I had been mobilised as a truck driver in a special transport command and after little or no training been sent with my unit to the eastern front and there I had been captured almost immediately by the Russians at Kalatch near Stalingrad. After being a prisoner of war in various camps on the Lena River in Siberia, I had been repatriated to Germany, owing to ill-health. My English accent was explained away by my English mother and the fact that in the Far East I had associated a lot with English people.

I remember that I objected to this story in respect to the time and place of my capture, for it appeared likely that if I said I had been captured near Stalingrad I might easily come in contact with one of the thousands of prisoners who had in fact been taken prisoner there and my story would then be exposed. The director told me not to worry about that as more than ninety per cent of the Stalingrad prisoners had died of typhus in Siberia.

The intention was that I was to live as a German in Berlin in order that I might acquire enough background to enable me later to pass as a German without doubt or question in the Argentine. I was to avoid any open political opinions and to have no connection, open or otherwise, with any sort of left-wing activity. In private I was to favour the extreme right wing and give vent to discreet pro-Nazi sentiments. This was with the object of trying to discover secret Nazis who would vouch for me in the Argentine. If necessary the Centre would facilitate their "escape" to the Argentine or America, and similar facilities would be extended to me. (In this connection it is perhaps interesting to speculate about the many stories of Nazi "escape routes" from Germany. The majority of these can probably be put down to journalists in want of a good story. It appears possible, however, that there may be a grain of truth in the heap of chaff and if so perhaps some of the routes have been organised by the Centre for purposes similar to mine.)

It was decided that I should stay in Berlin for at least six months and probably for a year, in order that I should merge completely into the postwar German background. The director assured me that all was laid on in Berlin and that on my arrival I would at once step into my German identity.

Late in February 1947 I left Sehjodnya and returned to Moscow. Here I was put through an intensive interrogation by the Political Department of the Centre in a last final checkup of my political reliability. All was apparently well, and I passed this, my final examination at the hands of the Russians, with flying colours.

There was one final banquet for me at which the director, Victor, and the chief political instructor of the Centre were present, and then one morning early in March I left Moscow for the airport and Berlin. I was travelling this time as Major Granatoff and was accompanied by a courier whose job was to steer me through the controls and customs in Moscow and Berlin and to ensure that all was done with the minimum of publicity.

As I flew over the endless, dreary wastes of Russia, at last travelling westward for the first time for over two years, I comforted myself with the thought that I had at least left the frying pan and was within measurable distance of being out of the fire. Unless unforeseen circumstances prevented it, or I bungled things at the last moment, there now seemed every chance that shortly I should be able to cut myself loose from the Centre forever.

20

BERLIN AND FREEDOM

It seemed reasonable to hope, after all the discussions and delays in Moscow regarding my assignment abroad, that when I finally arrived in Berlin something might have been done to enable me to take up my new role at once. Such hope was, however, in vain. The inefficiency of the Russian Intelligence Service in matters of detail and administration was a perpetual source of amazement to me. It would seem impossible to an ordinary person that a service run on such inefficient lines could ever achieve any results. Any ordinary intelligence service would have fiddled itself into inanition long ago. That the Red Army Intelligence continues to function and to function efficiently is due, I feel, far more to the efficiency of its agents and organisers in the field and to the facilities offered by the local Communist parties than to the driving and organising power of the Centre.

I was met at the Berlin airport by a Captain Smirnov, the Berlin representative of the Centre, who stated that though he had received instructions that I was to adopt the role of Albert Mueller at once he frankly had not the first idea of how to set about it. The Centre had stipulated, for obvious security reasons, that there must be no trace of Soviet help in obtaining my documentation, as this might be checked up by a future German government. Poor Smirnov did not know even how to begin on such a task. As a result I was given a flat at Grellenstrasse 12, in the Soviet Zone of Berlin, and lived there in my role as Major Granatoff.

After a series of talks with Smirnov, who could not have been pleasanter and could not possibly have had less idea how to set about things, it was obvious that if ever I was to get papers at all I would have to set about doing it myself. I therefore started off on the long and wearisome process of getting myself documented with no assistance, official or unofficial. For anyone trying to do the same thing in Berlin I can give the only two infallible ingredients for success: endless patience and an inexhaustible supply of cigarettes. With these two assets anything can be done in Berlin—in time.

My only documentary asset was a certificate of release as a prisoner of war which Smirnov did manage to supply. Each morning I started off on my tour of the municipal offices in the Soviet Zone and by the time I had achieved my object I had interviewed most of the officials in the bürgermeister's office, the Housing Office, the Labour Exchange, the Food Office, the Health Office, and of course the police. I had to get documents not only to prove that I was Albert Mueller but also to allow me to live in Berlin. The former was a great deal easier than the latter as Berlin was grossly overcrowded and many genuine Berliners who had been evacuated during the war were clamouring to come back, and they obviously had far more right to live there than did Mueller, a former resident of Riga. By design both Riga and my later notional domicile, Koenigsberg, were in Russian hands and the archives of the Wehrmacht, which would have shown a significant absence of any mention of Albert Mueller late of a transport command, were also in the hands of the Allies and not available to the German authorities.

Almost all the officials were new to their jobs, being former members of the Communist Party and former inmates of concentration camps. The procedure was for each official after hearing my story to pass me on to another official, a little higher up in the hierarchy, to whom I told the same rigmarole again. No one seemed to know quite what to do with a case like mine and I was indeed somewhat of a curiosity, as not many prisoners had then been returned to Germany from Russian camps. Each interview and each request for an interview was accompanied with a suitable *douceur* in the form of cigarettes.

I was invariably asked about my life as a prisoner of war and I always pitched a good, full-blooded horror story. All the officials were allegedly members of the S.E.D., the Communist-dominated German Unity Party, but the story was always very well received by these outward collaborators with the Russians. I was reminded of the old prewar anti-Nazi joke about a "Berlin steak" which was "brown outside and red inside." The roles were partially reversed. Soviet Berlin was a beautiful uniform red outside. The colour of the steak inside varied, but it was very seldom red all through.

Patience and cigarettes won through in the end and on April 12, 1947, I received my documents and was allocated a room in a flat belonging to Frau Weber, Wisbyerstrasse 41, Pankow. Up to this time I had been living the life of the destitute and homeless Mueller during the day, and at night returned to the sybaritic existence of Major Granatoff. The time had now come to discard Major Hyde and become permanently Herr Jekyll. Before doing so, however, I transferred to my new room all the food I had managed to bring with me from Russia or amass during my stay at Grellenstrasse. I had also been given thirty thousand marks as salary for a year but this was of little use as compared to my stock of food and cigarettes. I was determined before I finally left Russian service to have a short, final fling and had collected this food in order to have a holiday of a month or two.

Before I ceased to be Major Granatoff, part time, a place of conspiracy in Berlin had been arranged by Smirnov. In case the Centre wished to contact me I was to go on the last Sunday in every month to the Prenzlauer station, carrying a leather belt in one hand and my hat in the other. If the Centre wished to contact me someone would come up to me and say, "*Wann fährt der letzte Zug ab?* [When does the last train go?]" My reply was: "*Seit Morgen um 22 Uhr* [Since tomorrow at 10 p.m.]." If on the other hand I wanted to contact the Centre all I had to do was put a notice on a certain public notice board in Berlin reading: "*Suche Kinderfahrrad. A.*

Kleber Muristrasse 12, Berlin/Gruenau [Wanted, a child's bicycle]," and the next day an agent of the Centre's would come to the place of conspiracy at the Prenzlauer station. He would come straight up and say that he had seen the advertisement, for I would be known to him by sight as a result of my monthly visits. I went to the rendezvous once or twice and succeeded in identifying the Centre's agent but he never contacted me and I never tried to get in touch with him. For all I know he is still faithfully turning up there once a month.

These visits to the place of conspiracy were the last contacts I had with the Centre. I never saw Smirnov after that day in April when I at last got my documentation as Mueller complete. I lived for some time as Mueller in my little room in the Wisbyerstrasse. It was not uncomfortable there as it was on the top floor and comparatively undamaged and unlooted. The Russian soldiers principally confined their looting to the lower floors so the higher one was in any building the better. Life in the curious, twilight world of the defeated capital was not uninteresting but my experiences there have little bearing on this narrative and anyway enough has already been written about Germany in defeat.

The sun was shining on the ruins of Berlin when on August 2, 1947, I left the Russian sector and walked into the British Zone and freedom.

21

ENVOI

Now that it is all over and I am once again a private citizen in England, it is possible to look back and sum up these ten years of my life. I joined the International Brigade and fought in Spain partly because of a love of adventure and partly because I felt that the cause was right. I worked for the Red Army Intelligence Service from a love of adventure and partly because I was working against Fascism and the enemies of democracy. I left the service of the Russians because I realised that to continue working would be to work against freedom and for dictatorship.

I can look back on these ten years with no regrets. The fight in Spain failed because the enemies of the Republic were too strong and their friends too weak or too unwilling to realise that this was yet another step in the Nazi programme for world domination. The war against Fascism was successful because all the enemies of Fascism combined together in an all-out effort and my efforts with the Soviet spy ring in Switzerland contributed in some degree to the ultimate defeat of the Third Reich. With the war over and Fascism defeated and in ruins, it was obvious to me that a new danger to democracy had taken its place in the shape of Soviet Russia. The danger had been there all along but, with the defeat of Germany and Japan, Soviet Russia remained alone as the greatest threat to the peace of the world. As long as the Western democracies and Russia were fighting a common enemy, so long would Russia cooperate with the democracies and so long was it possible to justify working for Russia against the common enemy. As soon as that frail bond of a common purpose was shattered, then the Russian desire for "security," which bears a startling resemblance to what was called before the war "Nazi aggression," came to the fore and its sequel in eastern Europe is now history. To have continued after the war to act as a spy for Soviet Russia would have been to be a traitor to those principles for which I and many others fought, and many died, in Spain. When I went to Spain and during the war when I saw the magnificent way in which the Russians fought to save their Fatherland, it was possible still to believe in the ideas and ideals of Communism. After a period in Russia, and leisure to think back on the actions of Soviet diplomacy and politics in the past, it might have been possible to remain a theoretical Communist, but I found it quite impossible to believe in Communism as practised in Russia today.

The Nazis have been described, quite rightly so, and equally rightly held up to the execration of the world, as ruthless exponents of "Realpolitik" and "Machtpolitik." Russia has nothing to learn from Nazi Germany in this respect. The tactical methods of the Kremlin change with bewildering frequency and speed, the political sails trimmed to suit the prevailing breeze. The strategic aim remains steadily and unwaveringly the same. That aim has been as clearly described by Stalin as was the aim of National Socialism in *Mein Kampf*. The Comintern may be officially dead, but the ghost clothes itself, as soon as peace comes, in the flesh of the Cominform. The ultimate aim is still to spread Communism throughout the world. Such a spread, if successful, means in effect the spread of the power and control of Soviet Russia. It is only necessary to pick up a newspaper to see what that means: suppression of freedom of thought and speech; the power of the political police; purges; arrests and oppression. The picture is tragically familiar.

I remember during the course of my political instruction in Moscow hearing the Nazis being described as sentimentalists and thus totally unfitted to carry out their desire for world domination. As an example of this sentimentality I was told that in order

to liquidate a few thousand Jews in Salonika they had to be trans-
ported halfway across Europe to Auschwitz as the Wehrmacht refused to carry out executions on the spot. My instructor was interesting on the subject of the Jews, and showed to the full his Russian realism. He explained that the report of the Duke of Wellington
on the defeat of Napoleon in Russia could be equally applied to
Hitler. The duke had pointed out that the failure of Napoleon to
use the Jews as agents and go-betweens between his armies and
the Russians had led to his failure to exploit the Russian territory
that he had overrun. Only the Russian Jew was able to understand
and manage the Russian peasant. Hitler had made a similar mistake in liquidating rather than using the Jewish population in the
conquered Eastern territories. No horror was expressed at the ruthless extermination policy of the Nazis and the attendant horrors
of the concentration camps and the gas chambers. It was merely
coldly expressed as a statement of fact and as a proof of German
stupidity.

It is not for me to speculate as to the future of relations between the West and Russia. I am neither a politician nor a crystal-
gazer. It is also unnecessary for me to discourse at length on the
merits or demerits of Communism in theory and in Russian practice. It is perhaps pertinent to point out, however, that I started
my Civil War days believing that Communism might well provide
a solution to the ills of the world and ended by severing all connection with the Party and with Russia and retiring to the "decadent democracy" of England. I could have remained in Russian
service and might now be well established as an important agent
in their network working against the West; that I did not and preferred the uncertainty of life in England is proof enough of my
present feelings.

One thing I am perhaps qualified to sum up is the effectiveness and dangers of the Russian espionage service. It is obvious
that as long as the policy of Russia and her satellites is opposed to
the policies of the democracies so long will Russia attempt to discover the secrets of the West. It only remains to see how serious a
danger this is.

Throughout my narrative I have shown both the failures and the successes of the Red Army Intelligence Service. The faults were many and manifest. The Centre were frequently foolish, frequently uncooperative, and frequently inefficient. They were often dilatory when speed was essential and rash when caution was the better course. In fact the rigidity of the control and the lack of imagination of the Centre might lead one to assume that the dangers cannot be great if the system is so bad. Such an assumption would be dangerous in the extreme, as there is a great deal on the credit side, though much of it is imponderable.

Firstly, the Russian spy system has a ready-made network on the ground in the shape of the national Communist Party. This organisation provides a recruiting ground for agents, a source of funds and supplies, and, in time of war, a ready-made resistance movement. It cannot be sufficiently emphasised—and all accounts of trials of Soviet spies and reports of Soviet espionage have clearly shown it—that the loyalty of a Party member lies primarily with the Party and secondarily with his country. It is impossible to have a better recruit for espionage. As a result he is prepared to take enormous risks, work long hours for little pay, and live, and if necessary die, for the ideals of the Party, which means, in effect, for Moscow. It is from this overriding loyalty to Party rather than to patriotism that the Russian spy system derives its strength.

Secondly, though the organisation may break down on occasion, the system on which the various networks are run and the security regulations that are enforced on all members make the Russian network as safe as any from penetration by agents or action by counterespionage authorities. The failure of the Swiss network was due to lack of security precautions in Switzerland and the insistence of Moscow that it should keep running against their own security rules. A network in peacetime, carefully built up, is likely to continue to work efficiently and undiscovered. The Canadian organisation, hurriedly and badly organised as it was, was uncovered only by accident, and defectors like Gouzenko are few and far between.

The obvious and important question is whether there is a Russian spy net at work in England and America at the present moment. On that point I have no factual evidence and if I had I obviously could not give it here. On the other hand it would be safe to say that the odds are definitely in favour of networks existing both in England and the United States. I should imagine that the director has managed by now to rebuild his organisation in the States, which had gone underground at the time of the Canadian affair, and also has set up several new networks, though perhaps my defection has reduced their number by one. As regards England there was obviously some sort of organisation in existence there before the war, because I was recruited by it. I should imagine that it had now been revived and working again. If the Soviet espionage rules are being observed one would imagine that it was being directed from abroad and that the resident director for the English network was probably in France or Belgium. That there is a network busily engaged in Europe is obvious. If anyone disbelieves me all he has to do is tune his wireless in to the short-wave band. He may not be able to recognise, but I can, the characteristics of a Russian secret transmitter and the characteristics of their control stations. I often tune in and listen to the meaningless dots and dashes and wonder which network is on the air and whether it perhaps contains some of my old colleagues.

As regards my colleagues I think it unlikely that many of them are active. Rado is dead, his wife probably still in Paris unless she has been lured back; Cissie discredited; Sonia in retirement. But Lucy may have moved and be exercising his undoubted talents in some new field, and some of the other agents, known to me only by cover names, may still be engaged in the same work. The Centre is not idle and the new espionage school at Sehjodnya is unlikely to be empty. Time alone will show the effectiveness and extent of the new networks. I can only hope that the time may never come.

APPENDIX A

NOTES ON MY W/T CODE WITH MOSCOW

The process of enciphering messages for the Centre was divided into two parts. The first stage is comparatively simple and can easily be carried in the head, and, as I have stated, I frequently made notes in this First Stage Cipher for ease and convenience. The second stage involves the "closing" of the first simple encipherment against the text of a code book. (In this case, a "code book" is any ordinary published book that may be selected.)

The first stage of encipherment is based on a key word, which must have six letters and which is changed at intervals by the Centre. In the example to follow the key word is PLAYER. This is written out horizontally, and below it—in line—the remainder of the alphabet is written out (in the case of PLAYER in groups of six) together with a symbol for "signal" (@) and Full Stop. "Signal" means that the message changes over from letters to numbers.

At this stage the "pattern" looks like this:

```
P L A Y E R
B C D F G H
I J K M N O
Q S T U V W
X Z @ .
```

It is now necessary to assign a number to each letter, and for this purpose the numbers 1-9, 00-09, and 40-49 are used. (In the first set of numbers the figure 4 is omitted as it would lead to confusion with the double numbers beginning with 40.)

Those letters which are changed into single figures (1-9) are
ASINTOER (arranged in this order for mnemonic purposes), the
numbers being assigned to the relevant letters as they occur reading vertically and starting in the top left-hand corner of the diagram. With these numbers in place, the diagram now looks as follows:

```
    3   6 8
P L A Y E R

B C D F G H

1       7 9
I J K M N O

  2 5
Q S T U V W

X Z @ .
```

To this pattern are now added the double numbers (00-09, 40-
49), starting from the top left corner and going down the columns
consecutively filling in the blanks.

With all the numbers inserted, the diagram now looks like this:

```
00 04 3  41 6  8
P  L  A  Y  E  R

01 05 08 42 46 48
B  C  D  F  G  H

1  06 09 43 7  9
I  J  K  M  N  O

02 2  5  44 47 49
Q  S  T  U  V  W

03 07 40 45
X  Z  @  .
```

(This pattern is, of course, changed occasionally by the Centre
by allocating a different "mnemonic" or by changing the code word,
or both.)

A message enciphered in the first stage would look like this. (After a change from words to numerals, indicated by the symbol "signal," the numerals are each repeated three times.)

```
08 1 8  6 05 5 9  8 45 48 3 47  6  8  6 05 6  1 47 6 08
D  I R E C T  O  R . H  A  V E R E C E  I  V E D

41 9 44 8 7  8 2 45   40    666 888 45 666 999 45 777
Y  O U R N R S . (Signal) 6     8    .  6   9   .  7

000 40 45 06  1 43 45 7 8 45  40 444 111 40 45
 0  @  . J I M . N R . @  4  1  @  .
```

These figures are then split up into five-figure groups, the third and antepenultimate groups being left blank to take "recognition groups." At this stage the message begins to look like a ciphered message, but is still by no means secure and would present no difficulties to a cryptographer. Here it is with the blanks left for the recognition groups and the last group made up with noughts to complete a five-figure group.

08186	05598		45483	47686	05614
76084	19448	78245	40666	88845	66699
94577	70004	04506	14345	78454	04441
	11404	50000			

At this point the first stage of encipherment is complete. It is now necessary to "close" the message by re-enciphering it against the selected portion of the "code book." In practice, I used a Swiss book of trade statistics, but not having that by me now, I think it might be appropriate to take a passage at random from the report of the Royal Commission on the Canadian spy case.

On page 77, line 14, is the following phrase: "*that even if the adherent or member should refuse to engage in activities so clearly illegal and which constitute so clear a betrayal of his or her country.*"

The enciphering phrase can be taken from anywhere in the book, starting at any word in any line. In this case it starts at the fourth word of the line, i.e., "that."

From here on the key phrase is enciphered in exactly the same way as was the original message, and written out in five-figure groups, leaving here also the third and antepenultimate groups blank, as below:

54835 64767   14254 86308 48686 75984 36430

16824 89440 40886 42442 65967 46346 61730 55147

15162 29050   46380 44110

These groups are then added to the groups of the original ciphered message, the tens being ignored, and the final result is this:

	08186	05598			45483	47686
	54835	64767			14254	86308
	52911	69255			59637	23984
05614	76084	19448			78245	40666
48686	75984	36430			16824	89440
43290	41968	45878			84069	29006
88845	66699	94577	70004	04506	14345
40886	42442	65967	46346	61730	55147
28621	08031	59434	16340	65236	69482
78454	04441		11404	50000	
15162	29050		46380	44110	
83516	23491		57784	94110	

Now the message is complete save for the two recognition groups which enable the recipient to decipher the message. These are made up—in different ways—from the "code book group," the "fixed group," and the "message group."

The code book group is composed of the page number, line number, and word number of the key phrase. In this case, page 77, line 14, and word (from left) 4—77144.

The fixed group—69696—is given by the Centre and changed only on orders from the Centre.

The message group is, for the *first* recognition group, the *fifth* group of the message as enciphered so far, i.e., 43290; for the *second* recognition group, the message group is the *fifth* group from the end of the message as enciphered so far, i.e., 69482.

Now in each case the code book group, the fixed group, and the message group are added together. Thus:

	Recognition 1	*Recognition 2*
Code Book	77144	77144
Fixed Group	69696	69696
Message Group	43290	69482
	79920	95112

These two totals are now inserted in the appropriate spaces in the already enciphered message and the final result reads as follows:

52911 69255 79920 59637 23984 43290 49168 45878

84069 29006 28621 08031 59434 16340 65236 69482

83516 23491 95112 57784 94110

DECIPHERMENT

In decipherment, naturally, the first essential is to unravel the components of the two recognition groups. To illustrate this process clearly, let us recapitulate how the two recognition groups were arrived at. The first recognition group was composed of the code book group (C), the fixed group (F), and the fifth group of the enciphered message (not counting the blank) (M1); the second recognition group was composed of the code book group (C), the fixed recognition group (F), and the fifth group from the *end* of the enciphered message (not counting the blank) (M2). Therefore the first recognition group is made up of C+F+M1, and the second recognition group is made up of C+F+M2.

To break down the first recognition group, subtract from it the fixed group (69696—already known by agreement) (F), and the *sixth* group of the completed message (Ml), thus leaving C. The second recognition group is really only a cross-check, for on subtracting from it F and M2 the result should also be C.

Once C is known, the corresponding passage in the key book can be turned up, and the decipherment follows by using the reverse procedure of the encipherment.

Appendix B
Connections between the Swiss Network
and the Canadian Spy Case

The material upon which this Appendix is based is all available in the report of the Royal Commission with special reference to Section 6, pages 567-613, which section gives the interrogation of Hermina Rabinowitch. A serious student of the subject is recommended to refer to the report. This Appendix merely gives a shortened version of the evidence available in the report with my comments upon it. It is unnecessary here to quote in full the lengthy interrogation of Hermina Rabinowitch, which led up to the establishment of the Commission's conclusions.

There are five relevant documents concerning the connections between Canada and the network with which I was concerned in Switzerland. They are a four-page document written in Russian by Motinov (cover name "Lamont"), the assistant military attaché; a typewritten letter addressed to Rabinowitch and signed "Gisel"; a report in Russian on an interview between Koudriavtzev, First Secretary of the embassy (cover name "Leon"), and Rabinowitch; two reports on meetings between Koudriavtzev and Rabinowitch, and a typewritten letter from the latter.

The first document shows that in December 1943 Hermina phoned Tounkin, the counsellor of the Soviet Embassy in Ottawa, and asked to be received on an urgent matter. She was ultimately received by him and outlined to him the gist of the matter which she wished to discuss and after that she wrote him a letter on March 9, 1944, saying that she had received through a reliable channel a letter from a friend in Geneva. The contents of this letter are as follows:

205

We live in the former apartment and are working as previously in the old firm. Some two weeks
ago Sisi sent you a telegram. Tell us how did your
journey to Gisel's parents turn out. My health is excellent. Albert is sick and will probably leave his profession for a long time, he is laid up in bed. Relations with Lucy are good, she is a very good woman.
Gisel's family is for some reason no longer interested
in her, although up to this time there was support.
Lucy's situation has improved. Sisi's position is sad.
Please inform Gisel's parents that they must remit
6,700 dollars. This sum must be handed over
through you. There are no other possibilities. The
Gisels must bear these expenses. Advise me about
Aleksander where is he. Rachel.

It took the Royal Commission some time to unravel the meaning of this letter, and in some respects their deductions were in-
correct. Small blame attaches to the Commission on this point as
they were not in possession of the information regarding our network in Switzerland which is now available to the reader of this
book. Before considering the actual meaning of this letter it is as
well to remember the situation at the end of 1943 and the beginning of 1944. At this period the network was in a state of disor-
ganisation. Rado was in hiding; I was in prison, having been arrested in November 1943; contact with the Centre had been lost
and Cissie was without funds but was still receiving Lucy's information, for which she had to pay. With that background in mind it
is possible to analyse the message. "Working as previously in the
old firm" of course means that Cissie was continuing her work for
the Centre. Sisi is of course the same as Cissie, in other words
Rachel Duebendorfer. The reference to Gisel is obscure. According to Gouzenko, Gisel was a cover name for the Red Army Intelligence Service. This may be correct. On the other hand Gisel may
possibly be the cover name for some individual in the Centre who
may have been known not only to Cissie but also to Hermina. The

sentence, "Tell us how did your journey to Gisel's parents turn out" may well mean "How did you get on with the Russians in Canada?" The next sentences, "My health is excellent. Albert is sick and will probably leave his profession for a long time, he is laid up in bed," will present no difficulty to the reader, accustomed as he is to the jargon of the Centre. It is implied of course that Cissie is at liberty while Albert, i.e., Rado, was compromised and would probably have to cease being an agent for some time and was in hiding.

The next portion of the message referred of course to Selzinger (cover name Lucy), our source who supplied information from Berlin. "Relations with Lucy are good, she is a very good woman," i.e., "We are still receiving information from Selzinger, who is working well." "Gisel's family is for some reason no longer interested in her, although up to this time there was support. Lucy's situation has improved." That is to say, the Centre is for some reason no longer interested in information supplied by Lucy, although they had shown interest up to that time. The last sentence about Lucy's situation is somewhat obscure, but may mean that Selzinger was in a position to get even more information.

The next portion of the message was the one which in the Centre's view caused all the trouble. "Sisi's position is sad. Please inform Gisel's parents that they must remit 6,700 dollars. This sum must be handed over through you. There are no other possibilities. The Gisels must bear these expenses." This message is perfectly clear. Cissie's financial position was precarious and Hermina was to inform the Centre that they were to send $6,700 through Hermina, as there were no other means of obtaining money.

The last sentence, "Advise me about Aleksander where is he," is a sentence where I think that the Commission went somewhat astray. They identify Aleksander with Alexander A . . . whom I take to be Isaac, one of Cissie's sources in the I.L.O. It is not surprising that the Commission was confused, because Alexander A . . . is mentioned later, as he was the cut-out for this transaction. In point of fact I am certain that that Aleksander referred to in this sentence is myself. Cissie was unaware of my cover name Jim, and knew me only by my real name, which she had learnt from the members of the Abwehr who had visited her that summer and asked about me. It will be remembered that at this time we were not in touch as Rado had refused to allow us to meet, so she would have to refer to me by my real Christian name. At that early stage she would have been unaware that I was under arrest and might have thought that I was still in hiding. The signature "Rachel" is of course Rachel Duebendorfer.

Later on Hermina wrote again to Tounkin with a request that he should take action over the matter referred to in her first letter, i.e., the transfer of the funds, and to show the genuineness of the request she attached to this letter a second letter from Cissie of which the following is the gist:

> I have received your [Hermina's] telegram of
> 23.1.44. Please inform Gisel's family, that she should
> advise Znamensky 19, that Sisi is alive and works as
> of old with Lucy. Lucy wanted to change the person-
> nel, but funds ran out. Albert is sick and is not in-
> terested in business. For the work of Sisi, Gisel's
> family must transfer 10,000 dollars. The transfer
> must be made by Hermina personally through N.Y.
> in connection with the wishes of Mr. Helmars.
> R.D.

From this it appears that Hermina had replied to Cissie by tele-gram, presumably through the cut-out Isaac. Cissie then asked Hermina to inform "Gisel's family," i.e., the Russians in Canada, that they should inform Znamensky 19, which is the street address in Moscow of the Red Army Intelligence Headquarters, that Cissie was alive and continuing her work for the network. She was also working as before with Selzinger, who wanted to make a change of agents but funds had run out. Rado was in hiding and was not con-cerned with this operation. In this message Cissie increases her demand and asks now for $10,000 to be transferred by the Centre through New York. The initials R.D. which sign the letter are of course those of Rachel Duebendorfer.

As a result of this Pavlov informed Motinov and it was decided that she should be contacted by telephone and told she must not write or ring up, but that she would be visited in two weeks' time by a man from the Centre. This visit was in fact made by Koudriavtzev. It was considered by Motinov that the money should be transferred but that it must be transferred to Washington and then handed over to Hermina in New York as it was dangerous to cross the border with such a sum. Motinov added that Hermina's letters with copies of Cissie's letters had been sent by mail and in all probability had passed through the censorship. He was particularly concerned over the second letter quoted above and the mention of Znamensky 19, which he regarded as "particularly prejudicial."

Some time later, on May 5, 1944, Koudriavtzev went to Montreal and met Hermina and allowed her to read a letter addressed to her and signed Gisel. This letter was obviously taken back by Koudriavtzev as it was one of the documents produced by Gouzenko and is the second of the five documents mentioned above.

The letter is as follows:

> Dear Hermina
> Thank you very much indeed for your care in our affairs and we hope that you will help us in future. It is important for us to send a letter to Geneva to Sisi. Can you send this letter with a reliable man to whom you trust? All expenses will be paid. Please let us know about your proposals in this connection as soon as possible. Please inform us about delivery of your service mail to Geneva and why are you sure that it is not censored? Please wire to Rashel or Alexander that Gisel's parents are interested about the health of Sisi and Paul and that they will help them. We ask you to forward $10,000 to that watch company according to the Sisi's instructions. Make arrangements with our representative about forwarding of this sum of money to you in USA. All your personal expenses will be paid.

With best regards
Gisel

With our knowledge of the situation, this letter is also clear. In effect the Centre thanks Hermina for her assistance and hopes this will continue in the future. They add that it is important for them to get the money to Cissie and ask for Hermina's views as to how the transfer should be made. The reference to "your service mail to Geneva" refers presumably to official mail from the I.L.O. Office in Ottawa, where Hermina was employed, to the I.L.O. Office in Geneva, which as the I.L.O. had courtesy diplomatic privilege would not have passed through the censorship. The Centre asked Hermina to send a telegram to Rachel or Alexander. This Alexander probably does not refer to me but to Isaac, and this is where I think that the Commission became somewhat confused over the two Alexanders. The reference to the interest of the Centre in the "health of Sisi and Paul" is moderately clear. The Centre was obviously interested to know whether Cissie was still at large. It seems unlikely that the Paul is Paul Boetcher with whom Cissie was living, as Boetcher was not to my knowledge in the network. It probably therefore refers to another Soviet agent of Cissie's whose real identity is unknown to me.

The next document is a report of the interview between Koudriavtzev and Hermina, at which meeting she was shown the letter from Gisel. In this interview the latter stated that her correspondence with Geneva was carried on by means of letters and telegrams. The letters were sent as part of the I.L.O. mail and not subject to scrutiny, taking about three weeks to a month. Telegrams took only a few days. There is here in Paragraph 2 of the document a reference to Aleksander A . . . , who as I have already said is Isaac. Hermina went on to state that she was a good friend of Cissie's and had helped her but had previously not known anything about Cissie's work. She was completely certain that the letters had been written personally by Cissie as her handwriting and signature were well known to Hermina. At this interview Hermina stated that she would be able to send the money but would like it in a check as it was difficult to carry such large sums over the border in cash.

Koudriavtzev reported that Hermina's conduct throughout the meeting was natural. She stated during the meeting that her reception by Tounkin contrasted severely with her reception in Moscow, where she had been received warmly.

Hermina went to New York and handed over $10,000 to a watch company which had been previously known to Hermina when she was in Geneva.

The fourth document is a note by Motinov dated 31.7.44 in which it is stated that Koudriavtzev had met Hermina, who reported that she had handed over the money to the watch firm. She had subsequently sent a telegram to Isaac, who replied a few days later that he had not received the money. Koudriavtzev advised her to send another telegram to Isaac and one to the watch company. On 28.8.44 Koudriavtzev again met Hermina, who reported that she had not received confirmation from Isaac that he had received the money, but had received a telegram from the watch firm informing her that they had received a telegram from Isaac stating "thanks for the warm greetings." She therefore considered that the money had been received.

The last document is merely a letter from Hermina in which she states that she is enclosing a short memorandum on the I.L.O. and adding that she was at the disposal of the Russians for supplying any supplementary information as well as translation into Russian if required.

The above is of course a much abbreviated account of the minute investigation into the whole transaction which was undertaken by the Commission. In order not to make the reading of this Appendix too tedious I have not quoted the five documents in full but merely given the gist of them and those portions of them which refer to the connections with our network. Appendix C contains the five documents in full.

The other point of interest which emerges from the Commission's report is the reference to the use of Canadian passports. It will be remembered that when I first went to Moscow they were hoping to be able to supply me with a Canadian passport, but that as a result of the investigations by the Commission this proved impracticable. The Centre had informed me that anyway the obtaining of the passport would take time.

On page 41 of the report there is a reference to Canadian passports in a document from the dossier of Sam Carr removed by Gouzenko. This was a discussion between Colonel Milstein Milsky of the Red Army Intelligence Headquarters and Sam Carr. They met on 15.9.44 to discuss who prepared passports, i.e., what kind of people they were. Were they not old shoemakers who a few years ago fell through? That is to say that Milstein was anxious to know who was in a position to provide Canadian passports and whether this was the same organisation which had provided them in the past, which organisation had either been allowed to lapse or got broken up. Krivitsky also mentions the use of Canadian passports and an extract from his book is given on page 562 of the report in which he refers to the supplying of a Canadian passport to a Russian agent.

Appendix C

The following are the five documents quoted in the Royal Commission's report. (Underlining indicates words erased which have been recovered.)

I

HERMINA

R.H.—513 Grosvenor WA-lnut   3383
R.H.—6050 Darlington AT-lantic 3724
R.H.—4906 Queen Mary Rd. AT-   9148
14.4.44 Davie rang her up on these telephones but she was not there.

HISTORY

In December 1943 she rang up Tounkin and asked to be received on an urgent matter. T. refused, but afterwards received her. She outlined to him the gist of the matter. Tounkin inquired, but what she replied to him is not known. After that she wrote him a letter in which she wrote (9.3.44) that she had received through a reliable channel a letter from a friend in Geneva and attached it. The contents of the attached letter:

We live in the former apartment and are working as previously in the old firm. Some two weeks ago Sisi sent you a telegram. Tell us how did your journey to Gisel's parents turn out. My health is

213

excellent. Albert is sick and will probably leave his profession for a long time, he is laid up in bed. Relations with Lucy are good, she is a very good woman. Gisel's family is for some reason no longer interested in her, although up to this time there was support. Lucy's situation has improved. Sisi's position is sad. Please inform Gisel's parents that they must remit 6,700 dollars. This sum must be handed over through you. There are no other possibilities. The Gisels must bear these expenses. Advise me about Aleksander where is he. Rachel

After this Pavlov, 2nd Secr. neighbour, asked his boss who, according to Pavlov, allegedly replied that this is *their man* and you (Pavlov) should do nothing. At the same time he asked Pavlov for her address, which he did not and does not know. To Lamont's question why they did not inform us about this for so long, Pavlov replied, I had these instructions to do nothing. Not having received a reply to the letter and the inquiries by telephone 13 April, that is on the day of Davie's journey to Hermina's city, the latter wrote a second letter to Tounkin with a request to take measures in the matter of her first letter and for convincing she attached to this letter a second letter from Rachel of the following contents:

I have received your (Hermina's) telegram of 23.1.44. Please inform Gisel's family, that she should advise Znamensky 19 that Sisi is alive and works as of old with Lucy. Lucy wanted to change the personnel, but funds ran out. Albert is sick and is not interested in business. For the work of Sisi, Gisel's family must transfer 10,000 dollars. The transfer must be made by Hermina personally through N.Y. in connection with the wishes of Mr. Helmars. R.D.

Only after receiving this letter 15.4.44 did Pavlov 17.4.44 advise Lamont that there is a certain Rabinovich. After receiving these data on 19.4. we decided to contact her by telephone, as the letter was on her letterhead and to warn her that she must not write, nor ring up, and that in two weeks Gisel's man will visit her. <u>She was very satisfied</u> 19. This was carried out by Leon as Davie was in Vancouver. We consider that if there is to be a transfer of money, then the money be transferred to Washington and handed over to Hermina in New York, as it is dangerous to cross the border with such a sum. For one thing our banks are not releasing American dollars.

The letters with copies of Rachel's letters have been sent by mail by Hermina and in all probability passed through the censorship, although there was no censor's stamp. The copy of the second letter, which deals with Znamensky 19, was particularly prejudicial.

Please appoint a man for future procedure, bearing in mind that Davie will not be able to go to New York and Washington. I await instructions about the next meeting, also money. <u>We have</u>

Home telephone—Lancaster 7628

Business—Plateau 25.07

Address—Apt. 539 Pine Av. not far from University St.

(2 weeks from 19.4)

II

DEAR HERMINA,

Thank you very much indeed for your care in our affairs and we hope that you will help us in future. It is important for us to send a letter to Geneva to Sisi. Can you send this letter with a reliable man to whom you trust. All expenses will be paid. Please let us know about your proposals in this connection as soon as possible. Please inform us about delivery of your service mail to Geneva and why are you sure that it is not censored. Please wire to Rashel or Alexander that Gisel's parents are interested about the health of Sisi and Paul and that they will help them. We ask you to forward 10,000 dollars to that

watch company according to the Sisi's instructions. Make arrangements with our representative about forwarding of this
sum of money to you in USA. All your personal expenses will
be paid.

   With best regards
   Gisel

III

   On May 5 Leon met Hermina, the latter reported:
   1. The correspondence with Geneva is carried on by means
of letters and telegrams. The letters are sent as part of the mail
of her organisation and are not subject to scrutiny. The letters
take from three weeks to a month to come. Telegrams a few
days. The last letter took about one month to arrive, she does
not know the exact number of days.
   2. She knows not Geta A . . . but Aleksander A . . . She does
not correspond with him, but she could. She knows that everything is in order with him. She also informed that in June 1941
he intended to go to Moscow but the beginning of the war in-
terfered and he remained there. His visa was of 24 June.
   3. She knows Sisi as a good friend and she helped her as a
good acquaintance. She did not know anything about Sisi's work
previously. Sisi's first letter was for me unexpected. She knows
nothing of the change in Sisi's life.
   4. She is completely certain that the letters were written
personally by Sisi. Indications: handwriting and signature,
which were well known to her.
   5. The insistent request of Sisi to deposit the money in the
company was unknown to her, and furthermore she does not
know anybody in the said company. As for herself she considers that Sisi told the firm about me (Hermina).
   Hermina will be able to deposit the money, however she
would like to receive a cheque, as it is difficult to carry such a

large sum over the border. Hermina enjoys rights equal to persons who have diplomatic passports.

Conduct—natural. She wrote the letters to Tounkin because Tounkin had received her very severely once, while the other requests about a meeting and the telephone conversations were rejected, which sharply contrasts with my reception in Moscow where the reception was very warm.

She considers that there is no suspicion whatsoever about her. In her opinion letters sent from her town to our town appear to be not subjected to censorship.

The regular meeting was set for 17 of May, on May 20 she leaves for Philadelphia on her own office business and could take advantage of this journey as a good pretext, for handing over the money.

Appearance: A stout woman about 45 years, lame in both legs, moves with the aid of two sticks, but at the same time drives her own car.

Conclusion: The meeting under the cover of both contacts passed entirely normally.

I request your further directives.

6.5.44 Lamont

IV

31.7.44. Leon met Hermina, the latter reported that she had handed over the money to the owner of the firm, but he did not know anything about this money. After this she sent a telegram to A . . . and a few days later he answered her that he had not received the money. Leon advised her to send another telegram to A . . . and one to the owner of the firm.

Regular meeting on 1 or 4.9.44 at 21 (possibly 15). Leon has the time of the meeting smudged. On McTavish St.

Task—the characteristics of the institution.

28.8.44. Leon met Hermina, the latter reported that she had not received confirmation from A . . . about receipt of the money, but she received a telegram from the head of the firm in New York, who advised that he had received a telegram from A . . . with the contents "Thanks for the warm greetings." She considers that the money has been received. At the present time it does not seem possible to send a man to Geneva. There is no reliable man and link with Geneva.

Address of A . . .

Business: Geneva International Labour Office.

Home: Chemin . . . Geneva.

Regular meeting 28.9 at 9.00 (21) McTavish St.

V

Enclosed a short memorandum on the International Labour Organisation. I am entirely responsible for the views expressed in it. They are based on a long experience in the I.L.O. and on personal knowledge of most of the members of the staff.

I am, of course, at your disposal for any supplementary information as well as for the translation into Russian. Enclosed also a certain number of annexes.

Hermina Rabinowitch

August 20, 1944

COACHWHIP PUBLICATIONS

COACHWHIPBOOKS.COM

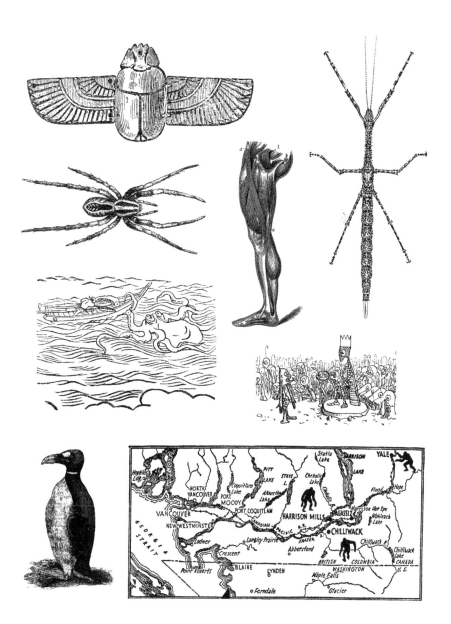

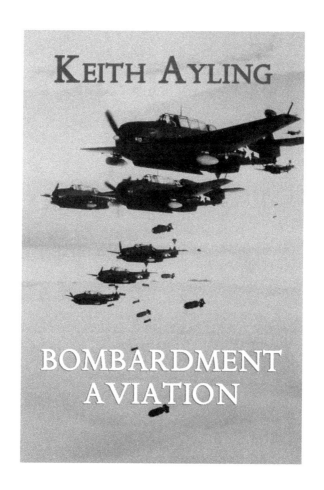

BOMBARDMENT AVIATION

ISBN 1-61646-054-7

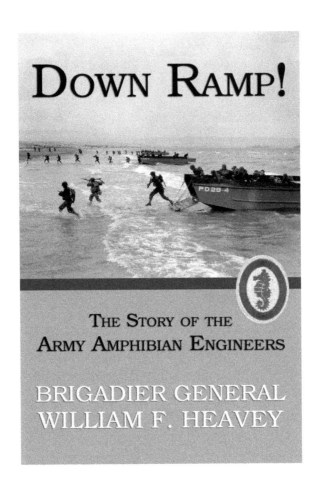

DOWN RAMP!

THE STORY OF THE
ARMY AMPHIBIAN ENGINEERS

BRIGADIER GENERAL
WILLIAM F. HEAVEY

DOWN RAMP!

ISBN 1-61646-057-1

BASTOGNE

The Story of the First Eight Days
In Which the 101st Airborne Division Was
Closed Within the Ring of German Forces

COLONEL S. L. A. MARSHALL

BASTOGNE

ISBN 1-61646-062-8

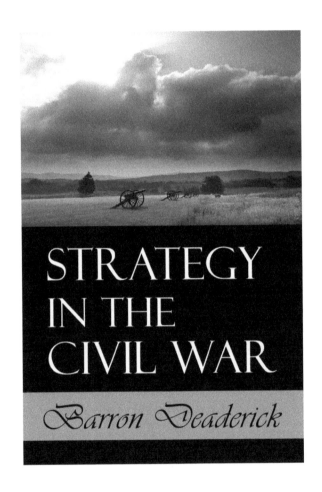

STRATEGY IN THE CIVIL WAR

ISBN 1-61646-064-8

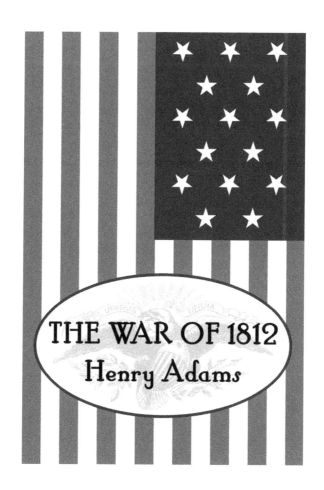

THE WAR OF 1812

ISBN 1-61646-065-5

CPSIA information can be obtained
at www.ICGtesting.com
Printed in the USA
BVHW03s1919040418
512493BV00001B/6/P